Praise for

SAINT GERMAIN'S
PROPHECY FOR THE NEW MILLENNIUM

"Terrific—a must read! This exciting blend of astrological, historical and spiritual perspectives is a fantastic guide for navigating the coming era. It gives us much-needed knowledge, strength and spiritual tools to help us move into the new millennium and shape the future we want. Well written, well researched and very empowering."

—DANNION BRINKLEY, author of *Saved by the Light*

"On the eve of the millennium, Elizabeth Clare Prophet reminds us that by our heartfelt connection with Spirit, in deed and thought, we can bring about the staying of the hand of darkness and bring on an Aquarian age of unprecedented light."

—JESS STEARN, author of *Edgar Cayce on the Millennium*

"You will love this book!"

—MAGICAL BLEND MAGAZINE

SAINT GERMAIN'S
PROPHECY
FOR THE NEW
MILLENNIUM

*Includes dramatic prophecies from
Nostradamus, Edgar Cayce and Mother Mary*

ELIZABETH
CLARE PROPHET

with PATRICIA R. SPADARO *and* MURRAY L. STEINMAN

SUMMIT UNIVERSITY 🕊 PRESS®
Corwin Springs, Montana

SAINT GERMAIN'S PROPHECY FOR THE NEW MILLENNIUM
*Includes dramatic prophecies from Nostradamus, Edgar
Cayce and Mother Mary* by Elizabeth Clare Prophet with
Patricia R. Spadaro and Murray L. Steinman
Copyright © 1999 by Summit University Press

For information, contact
Summit University Press, PO Box 5000, Corwin Springs, MT
59030-5000. Tel: 1-800-245-5445.
E-mail: info@summituniversitypress.com
Web site: www.summituniversitypress.com

Library of Congress Catalog Card Number: 99-60919
ISBN: 0-922729-45-X

SUMMIT UNIVERSITY 🕊 PRESS®
Summit University Press and 🕊 are registered trademarks.
Printed in the United States of America
05 04 03 02 01   7 6 5 4 3

Contents

Note: Because gender-neutral language can be cumbersome and at times confusing, we have used *he* and *him* to refer to God or the individual and *mankind* to refer to people in general. These terms are for readability only and are not intended to exclude women or the feminine aspect of the Godhead. God is both masculine and feminine.

Preface

In the middle of difficulty
lies opportunity.
—ALBERT EINSTEIN

Prophecy is a mixed bag. Seers of ancient and modern times say the new millennium can be a time of tremendous spiritual and technological progress, a time when we break free from the past—or it can be a time of war, turmoil and even cataclysm.

But one thing is for sure—we are in a time of unparalleled opportunity. We are at one of those great turning points in history when we can create a future that will ennoble mankind for ages to come.

This book can help you make the most of this opportunity. It brings together historical, astrological and spiritual perspectives that put prophecy, and our future, into context. Part I explores some of the most compelling prophecies of Nostradamus, Edgar Cayce, Mother Mary and Saint Germain for the coming years. It also explores major astrological cycles, which paint a picture of our future challenges and opportunities.

Part II talks about spiritual solutions and how we can transform our tomorrows by applying accelerated spiritual techniques. For there are always two ways of looking at the future. The first: the future is something that happens to you. The second: the future is in flux and can be shaped until the very moment it becomes a reality.

John Glenn once said, "People are afraid of the future, of the unknown. If a man faces up to it, and takes the dare of the future, he can have some control over his destiny. That's an exciting idea to me, better than waiting with everybody else to see what's going to happen."

We are all on stage, and each of us gets to choose the part we will play—how we will take on "the dare of the future." If we accurately read the signs of the times and apply our spiritual resources in the most practical way, I believe we together can shape the future we want.

PART I

Signs of the Times

*The future enters into us
in order to transform itself in us
long before it happens.*

—RAINER MARIA RILKE

A Sneak Preview

*My interest is in the future because
I am going to spend the rest of my life there.*
—CHARLES F. KETTERING

As we together write the first chapters of the twenty-first century, we are still searching for answers to many questions. Will the prophecies concerning war, earth changes and plagues come to pass? Will we find ourselves in chaos as a result of a global economy in flux? As technology accelerates, will our society become irreparably split into an elite of technological haves and an underclass of technological have-nots? Will terrorism become even more of a threat? Will we discover cures for diseases like cancer and AIDS, or will they continue to snuff out promising lives?

Some who claim to read the pages of our future history are prophets of doom and gloom. Others see only the potential for a bright new world. I believe we must look at the future as realists. I see the handwriting on the wall, but I also see a unique solution to our dilemma that can help us turn the new millennium into a golden age.

We will not be writing on a clean white page as we begin this new era. We will bring with us our past. Every day, in big ways and small, we are reaping the consequences of our past. The new millennium will be no different. The circumstances of our lives will be the result of our past actions—our karma.

Prophecy is, in fact, a sneak preview of the karma that will be returning to our doorstep for resolution. The prophets see where we are headed as a result of events we have set in motion, and they warn us of what's coming up if we don't change course. And therein lies the key.

Heaven has allowed the prophets a rare glimpse of what the future may hold so that we can transmute our negatives before the handwriting in our book of life becomes an indelible record and we reap the full consequences of our actions.

Simply put, *prophecy is mercy. Prophecy is opportunity. Prophecy is not set in stone.*

Can Prophecy Fail?

When I appeared on *Larry King Live* in 1990, I found that Larry shared the misconception many people have about prophecy—that once a prediction is given, the outcome cannot be changed. Here's an excerpt of our conversation:

Larry King: I guess what confounds people is, if your prophecy is ordained, what's the difference whether we believe or don't believe?

Elizabeth Clare Prophet: Well, I don't believe in predestination.... But I think that the prophets come to warn us that if we don't do certain things and come close to God, obey his laws and prepare, certain calamities may come upon us.

LK: But that, then, always allows you to say, "Well, we did good, so the prophets were wrong." In other words, the prophets can't be wrong. I could prophesy the end of the world next Saturday unless we're good, and then all I've got to do next Saturday is say we were good.

ECP: Well, I didn't make the rules, Larry. That's exactly what some of the Old Testament prophets did. And when the people received an awakening to their God and became close to him, the prophesied calamities did not fall upon them....

I don't think prophecy is final until it happens, ever, because of free will.... There is always hope.

But karma brings the circumstance of its return. And if people don't change, then it's pretty clear that the karma they have sown is what they're going to reap.

Earth Is a Crossroads

Our understanding of prophecy wouldn't be complete without first putting prophecy, and the future, into a historical and spiritual context. To understand the full picture, we must go back into the distant past—back beyond the reckoning of modern historians.

The story of earth is a complex one, one where the truth is sometimes stranger than fiction. Like an intricate novel woven with many plots and subplots, what we face today is the crisscrossing of many karmic patterns.

Some chapters of our ancient history tell of vast golden-age civilizations on the lost continents of Lemuria and Atlantis. Many of us lived there in previous incarnations and may have a soul memory of these times when we were guided by masters and adepts of great attainment. We knew the laws of the universe and applied them. We were spiritually developed. We enjoyed a quality of life far superior to what we have today.

We may also have an inner awareness of a time

when, under the influence of fallen angels, we betrayed our spiritual mentors. This is where the plot thickens.

Earth is a crossroads. It has been home to good, sweet and beautiful people. It has also hosted rebel angels and those influenced by them—those who did not use their talents and free will to do good and help others.[1]

The records and artifacts of ancient Sumer, Egypt, India and even the Incan civilization bear witness to these visitors. With their advanced knowledge of science and technology, they taught the arts of war. They bred deception, greed and allegiance to the ego. In the chronicles of earth's history, their dark threads of infamy are subtly interwoven with golden threads sown by the good people of earth.

Influenced by these cosmic rebels, the civilization of Lemuria experienced a decline. Her people, who once walked and talked with God's representatives, lost their native spiritual vision and abilities. This spiritual decline, coupled with misuses of power, the abuse of technology, and the unbridled pursuit of pleasure and the ego, resulted in the sinking of Lemuria many thousands of years ago. Today, all that remains of Lemuria is the Ring of Fire, the ring of volcanoes on the boundaries of the Pacific Ocean along the west coast of the Americas and the east coast of Asia.

After the downfall of Lemuria, another golden-age civilization arose on the ancient continent of Atlantis. In his dialogues, Plato recounts that on "the island of Atlantis there was a great and wonderful empire" that ruled Africa as far as Egypt, Europe as far as Italy, and "parts of the continent" (thought to be a reference to the Americas).

There came a time on Atlantis, too, when many people abandoned their first love and their allegiance to the divine light within. Their scientists even went so far as to create grotesque forms by interbreeding man and animals through genetic engineering. The half-man, half-goat forms we read about in mythology are a soul memory of these events. The once-great continents of Lemuria and Atlantis now lie beneath the oceans, their triumphs and their failures buried deep in the unconscious of the race.

Nothing Happens by Chance

Since then, the ages have rolled on like cars on a giant Ferris wheel. Civilizations have risen and flowered, then declined and disappeared. The people of Lemuria and Atlantis have reincarnated again and again throughout these civilizations, making good and bad karma along the way. Many have gravitated to the Americas. It is against this backdrop that you and I are about to take our place on the stage of cosmic history.

As we enter the new millennium, we the citizens of planet earth face not only our own personal karmic equations, but also world karma born of the interplay of many forces. It is a complex tapestry. Once again we are faced with ultimate choices. Will we sustain the connection to our spiritual roots that in the past allowed us to create golden-age communities? Or will we fall prey to the brittle intellect and the hardened heart, to materialism and worldly sophistication?

Some believe that the new millennium will be a golden age no matter what. That thesis doesn't take into account our free will. The actions we take will determine the course of our lives and the lives of future generations. The new era will become a golden age only if we make that golden age a reality.

Nothing in the universe happens by chance or by wish. No one else can do it for us, not the saints or adepts, not those who have lived before, not those who will live in the future. We must play our parts— parts that we have been waiting lifetimes to play.

How We Can Change the Future

Some of the best examples of how we can change the future and how prophecy can fail come from the wisdom of the ancients and the characters portrayed in the world's scriptures, like Jonah. And what a character he was!

In a comic sort of way, his story teaches us an invaluable lesson about prophecy. Scholars believe that the author of the Old Testament's Book of Jonah used the figure of Jonah, a historical eighth-century B.C. prophet, in a parable designed to expose the Jews' intolerant attitude toward their Gentile neighbors.

The narrative opens with God's commission to Jonah: "Up! Go to Nineveh, the great city, and inform them that their wickedness has become known to me."[2] Instead of heading toward Nineveh, which was the capital of the Assyrian empire, the prophet took off in the opposite direction and boarded a ship sailing for Tarshish.

Why did Jonah resist his assignment? The heathen Assyrians had been the cruel enemies of the Jews. Jonah feared that if he warned the people of Nineveh of God's wrath, they might turn from their evil ways and God might not punish them. Simply put, Jonah did not want God to save Nineveh. At one point in the drama, Jonah confesses to God: "That was why I went and fled to Tarshish: I knew that you were a God of tenderness and compassion, slow to anger, rich in graciousness, relenting from evil."

Jonah's attempted escape to Tarshish was futile.

A violent storm threatened the ship and its passengers. When the sailors cast lots to see who on board was responsible for bringing the anger of the gods upon them, the lot fell on the disobedient prophet.

Realizing that he was to blame, Jonah admitted to the sailors that he was trying to escape from God and told them that if they wanted to calm the sea, they should go ahead and throw him overboard. They did so reluctantly and the storm subsided. A "great fish" swallowed Jonah and he remained in its belly for three days and three nights until the fish vomited him onto dry land.

God again commanded his prophet to preach to the people of Nineveh, and this time Jonah obeyed. "Only forty days more and Nineveh is going to be destroyed," he cried out to the people. The warning hit its mark. Everyone in Nineveh, from the greatest to the least, fasted, put on sackcloth (which signified their state of mourning) and prayed that God would change his mind.

The king even took off his robe, put on sackcloth and sat down in ashes. "Let everyone renounce his evil behavior," the king proclaimed, "and the wicked things he has done." The people's stunning about-face worked: "God relented: he did not inflict on them the disaster which he had threatened."

The Lesson of the Unconsolable Prophet

Jonah, however, was indignant that the Ninevites had taken his advice and that his prophecy had failed. He begged God to take away his life and told him, "I might as well be dead as go on living." Jonah built himself a shelter on the east side of the city, sat down and waited to see what would happen.

God caused a gourd (castor-oil plant) to grow up to shade the forlorn prophet. Then the next day God sent a worm to attack the plant and it withered. As the sun beat down on Jonah's head and a scorching east wind blew, he again begged for death. He boldly told God that he was angry with him for destroying the plant.

The Book of Jonah ends abruptly as God unmasks Jonah's self-pity and bigotry: "You are only upset about a castor-oil plant which cost you no labor, which you did not make grow, which sprouted in a night and has perished in a night. And am I not to feel sorry for Nineveh, the great city, in which there are more than a hundred and twenty thousand people who cannot tell their right hand from their left, to say nothing of all the animals?"

Forty days of fasting was hardly enough for the people of Nineveh to make up for the gross misdeeds that had compelled God to threaten their destruction. But they showed good faith, and that was enough for God. The Book of Jonah carries such a strong message of the power of repentance that it is read publicly in its entirety on the Jewish holiday of Yom Kippur (the Day of Atonement).

The powerful lesson we can learn from this parable is that *prophecy is not set in stone.*

Most of the prophets of old were not as successful as Jonah was. Their warnings went unheeded, their prophecies came true, and the people received the full impact of the returning karma for their past misdeeds.

Astrological Ages

In coming chapters, we will explore what seers such as Nostradamus, Edgar Cayce, Mother Mary and Saint Germain have revealed for the coming millennium. First, let's take a look at another potent indicator of the future—astrology.

The birth of the new millennium coincides more or less with what is known as the age of Aquarius. What exactly is the Aquarian age? There are twelve astrological ages, each about 2,150 years long, and they take their names from the signs of the zodiac. An entire cycle of twelve ages spans about 25,800 years.

New ages are related to the "precession of the equinoxes." In astronomy this is the slow backward rotation of the earth around its polar axis. During this rotation, the point of the spring equinox moves through the signs of the zodiac, denoting which age we are in.

While no one knows exactly when each age begins or ends, we do know that we are in the waning days of the age of Pisces. Because of the precession, we move through the ages in reverse order. Prior to the age of Pisces, we were in the age of Aries and before that, the age of Taurus, and so on. In each age, we are destined to assimilate a certain attribute of God and develop it to its fullest potential.

The age of Aries, for example, brought the awareness of God as the Father, the Lawgiver. This age was characterized by God's direct communion with Moses. Moses showed us that we too could walk and talk with the indwelling Presence, the I AM THAT I AM. During the Arian age, the Egyptian pharaoh Ikhnaton also attained mystical union through his adoration of the one he called "Aton," symbolized as the sun.

The age of Pisces gave us the understanding of God as the Son, exemplified by the sponsor of that age, Jesus. Jesus' mission for the Piscean age was to be our mentor on the path of self-mastery and to show us what we could become. We learn from his example what we ourselves could have, and should have, attained during these 2,000 years of the Piscean age in preparation for the Aquarian age.

The Birth of a New Age

The dawning age of Aquarius brings us the awareness of God as the Holy Spirit and as the Divine Mother. In this age, both man and woman are destined to develop their feminine side—the creative, intuitive, nurturing and compassionate side of their soul.

The prophets say that Aquarius can be an age of freedom, peace and enlightenment, a time of technological progress combined with spiritual development. It can be a time when we break free from the past. It can be a time when the spirit of cooperation becomes the basis of every relationship—cooperation between God and humanity, and between people everywhere. Yet seers have also foreseen earth changes, war and turmoil.

What makes the Aquarian age such a turning point is that in order to fully enter that age, we must first face a karmic summing up. The negative karma of those who live on earth has been held in abeyance for thousands of years by the spiritual consciousness of the great lights of East and West. The end of the age of Pisces marks the day when we must carry the full momentum of our past karma, which is why the prophecies for this time of transition are so very sobering. We indeed carry the burden of history, and it is a heavy karmic burden.

Astrology—a Picture of Potentials

Like the writings of the prophets, the astrological handwriting in the skies shows the potential for great advances as well as great darkness. But again, prophecy as well as astrology is not set in stone. Astrological portents are indicators of what *might* come to pass if we don't change our ways.

Roger Bacon, the first modern scientist, made this point well over 500 years ago. He believed it was possible to avoid war through the study of astrology. Bacon said that if Church leaders had read the astrological warnings—such as the comet of 1264, which preceded the battles that broke out all over Europe—they might have averted the wars of their times.[3]

Astrology paints a picture of potentials based on the karmic material drawn from our many appearances on the stage of life. According to the law of karma, all the causes we have set in motion in the past, both good and bad, will return to us. Astrology tells us *when* that positive and negative karma will return and what shape it is likely to take.

But our astrology and our karma are only part of the drama. At center stage is our own free will. How will we react to the returning karma? Will we accept responsibility for our actions? Will we learn from the lessons of the past and move forward? Or will we repeat the same mistakes?

How we answer these questions will determine our destiny, not the configurations in the skies. As Shakespeare wisely observed, "The fault, dear Brutus, is not in our stars, but in ourselves."

The remainder of this chapter takes a look at three major astrological cycles that are already in effect and what they portend. In chapter 5 we will expand our horizons and look at what we can expect through 2025.

Pluto in Sagittarius: A Dramatic Transformation

What, then, does the current astrology tell us? First, let's examine the twelve-year transit of Pluto in Sagittarius that will conclude in 2008. During this cycle, we can expect momentous changes in religion and government, our values and beliefs, our education and culture. We will see a dramatic transformation in the vision we hold of ourselves, the world, our place in the universe and our relationship to God.

In the past, the transit of Pluto in Sagittarius coincided with the golden age of Pericles in Greece, the mission of Jesus Christ, the Italian Renaissance and the Enlightenment in Europe. It saw the introduction of Buddhism into central China and Christianity into Saxony. It coincided with the first unification of China and the codification of law in the sixth-century Roman Empire and in eleventh-century Russia.

Adventure, discovery and vision were on the march. The Portuguese reached China by sailing around the Cape of Good Hope. Roger Bacon predicted the invention of the steamship, the airplane and television. The Sorbonne was founded in Paris, and many cathedrals and temples were built in Europe and Asia.

This cycle also coincided with great religious conflict. Jesus was crucified and John the Baptist was beheaded. The Roman emperor Diocletian unleashed his notorious persecution of Christians. In Athens, Plato's school of philosophy was shut down because of its so-called pagan ideas. In Persia, Mani was executed for claiming he was a prophet who received divine revelations. In Europe, Germans persecuted "heretics" and Martin Luther led the Protestant Reformation.

The cycle of Pluto in Sagittarius also coincided with war—war over the control of the oracle of Delphi, the Second Peloponnesian War, the Second Punic War and the Seven Years' War.

Enlightenment or Repression?

What does all of this mean for us? It tells us that the current transit of Pluto in Sagittarius, like the previous ones, can have both positive aspects and negative aspects.

Between now and 2008, we can give birth to an age of enlightenment and to a new world religion. We must, however, anticipate a counterforce to this progress—the repression of religions and new ideas and even the possible outbreak of religious wars.

This twelve-year cycle could be a time of optimism and expansion. We could see appreciation of foreign cultures and advances in education. Information and culture will move across borders as never before. We may be richer for the experience, but we could also see cultures in conflict—conflict of the kind that has taken place in Bosnia, Rwanda and the Middle East. We could also see education denied to people or used to indoctrinate and control them.

Samuel Huntington, a professor of government at Harvard, argues that in the near future there will be a major clash of cultures. The West will be confronted by Asia in economic matters and by Islam in matters of religion.[4] With Pluto in Sagittarius there is the potential for increased conflict among different ethnic, religious and racial groups. Persecution along class or ethnic lines could cause mass migrations, with unpredictable results. The question of immigration will be debated in many nations. Some will accept refugees, others will not.

The cycle of Pluto in Sagittarius will set the stage for a transformation of governments and even the nature of government itself. Empires and groups of nations are likely to expand and, as they come into conflict with each other, be destroyed or reconfigured.

This could be a time of political ferment like the one that preceded the American and French revolutions. A new world order could take shape. New powers could emerge. And we will finally be forced to settle the question that dominated most of the twentieth century: Can the world exist half slave and half free?

The astrological indicators tell us that a political system of freedom or one of tyranny and chaos will begin to coalesce. The political culture developed during this cycle will begin to crystallize into the dominant form of government that will be established during the transit of Pluto in Capricorn, the sixteen-year cycle that runs from 2008 to 2024.

Uranus in Aquarius: Impulse for Freedom, Potential for War

The second important astrological cycle is the transit of Uranus (the planet of freedom) in Aquarius (the sign of freedom). Uranus will stay in Aquarius until 2003 and will be joined by other slow-moving planets during that time. The combination of these planets and the transit of Pluto in Sagittarius have much to do with the inauguration of the age of Aquarius.

These planets can give us the impulse for freedom, a transcendent spirituality and a sense of brotherhood. We could find new solutions to our many social problems and dissolve the barriers that divide us by religion, race, nationality, class and gender.

Yet we must be careful how we "fix" the social order. The last two times Uranus was in Aquarius were periods of war and revolution. There were revolutions and independence movements in Europe and South America. Slavery was abolished in Mexico and the British Empire, and the movement to abolish slavery gained power in the United States.

While these events were momentous, they are overshadowed in the pages of history by two conflicts that caused millions of deaths and changed the course of history—the Russian Revolution and World War I.

When two cycles coincide that portend war, as do Pluto in Sagittarius and Uranus in Aquarius, it is dangerous—especially today, given that more nations are developing nuclear-weapons capability and the Y2K problem heightens the potential for an accidental nuclear launch. Even more ominous is the fact that other powerful cycles between 1998 and 2001 also portend war, even a world war.

Past transits of Uranus in Aquarius have also coincided with great scientific discoveries and technological progress. Einstein, for example, formulated his general theory of relativity during such a transit. Today we are on the verge of making another great technological leap.

Imagine a world without television or computers, a world in which man had never traveled to the moon or launched a satellite, a world where man had not split the atom or unlocked the DNA code, a world without the Internet.

These scientific and technological advances all took place during the last complete transit of Uranus through the zodiac. It is from this base of knowledge that we will launch the next revolution in science—a revolution in microelectronics and microbiology, in computer science, information science, military science and communications technology.

The scientific breakthroughs of the coming decades could greatly improve the quality of life for us all, bringing greater wealth and leisure, longer life and robust health. These breakthroughs could also help launch a real revolution in education.

New Discoveries, New Powers

New discoveries bring new powers. To enable us to use these powers wisely and well, we will need a commensurate spiritual revolution. And we will have to decide, in our lifetime, where to draw the line—the line between what we can do and what we should do.

Scientists have already cloned mice and sheep. They have genetically engineered pigs and cows to bear human genes. They have grown a human ear on the back of a mouse. It was this kind of genetic manipulation taken to extremes that led to the sinking of Atlantis. The message: Man cannot play God.

Technology is a two-edged sword. It can imprison just as easily as it can liberate.

Will we use new communications technology to educate and inform? Or will we use it to control people and deprive them of their privacy? Will we decide that people with defective genes shouldn't be allowed to procreate, or even to be born?

In addition to the technological challenge, we will also face a social challenge. Because of our scientific progress, we are on the verge of permanently dividing societies into those who understand technology and those who do not. If that happens, the technological elite will control the wealth and power, and the technological have-nots will become a permanent underclass. That is a formula for disaster.

To summarize, during the transit of Uranus in Aquarius, we will have to decide how we are going to use our freedom. We are compelled to change and grow, but we must also avoid anarchy. We must avoid revolution along the lines of the Russian Revolution, which promised freedom but delivered tyranny and stifled the human spirit. And if we are going to have Godlike scientific powers, we must develop the Godlike wisdom to use them.

Neptune in Aquarius: The Democratization of Spirituality

The third major astrological cycle affecting us is the transit of Neptune (the planet of spirituality, self-transcendence and illumination) through Aquarius (the sign of freedom as well as brotherhood and egalitarian political movements). Neptune will be transiting through Aquarius until 2012.

Neptune dissolves or breaks down boundaries, which can lead to a greater sense of connection between countries and peoples and between ethnic, religious and social groups. Neptune brings feelings of idealism and new visions. It also carries the potential for disillusionment, uncontrolled mass movements, confusion, a general condition of depressed immune response and the rise of epidemics.

The most significant characteristic of the transit of Neptune in Aquarius is the democratization (or mass expression) of spirituality—spirituality for everyone. It can give us a new and higher way of looking at the world and at ourselves, a way to transcend our former environment. Today, for instance, we are seeing phrases and concepts in popular culture that even five years ago were not a part of common parlance, words like *karma, reincarnation, chakras.*

Another way of looking at Neptune in Aquarius is that it gives us the opportunity to achieve a higher level of community based on spiritual principles but manifest in a very practical manner. This noble goal is not without its risks. If we aren't able to manifest the elevated qualities of freedom and idealism, then this transit could produce a false sense of freedom, disillusionment, confusion, social disorganization, and in extreme cases anarchy or revolution.

When both Neptune and Uranus are in the sign of Aquarius, we can see experimentation and innovation, a new way of connecting with people around the world, a new way of looking at things and communicating information. We can see a new social consensus and the development of a new social contract between the society and its people.

Uranus and Neptune were last together in Aquarius in 1834 and 1835. As author Laurie Baum notes, this coincided with several notable events, including boundary wars in Europe, the secession of Texas from Mexico, the opening of the Western frontier, and the birth of modern medicine. She says all of these reflect a common desire to "go beyond circumscribed societal limits, to follow a new vision, to let go of the old way, and to be independent and free to experiment with the new."[5]

Beating the Fates

As we can see, the astrology for the coming years shows the magnificent potential for a golden age. It also shows that darkness can ensue if we sit back and do nothing. How can we bring in an age of enlightenment? What can we do to beat the Fates?

Enter Saint Germain, sponsor of the Aquarian age and great luminary of the twenty-first century. He brings a vast historical perspective and a deep understanding of the challenges that we all must face.

Saint Germain comes with a solution to the problems of our very ancient, very complex karma—a high-frequency spiritual energy that can transmute (transform) negative karma into positive energy. Although he is a master alchemist, Saint Germain's solution is only good if we run with it, for once karma crystallizes it is much harder to turn back.

I firmly believe that in the face of any and all negative predictions, we the people of earth—applying our highest wisdom and our deepest compassion, our material resources and our practical spirituality—can make these prophecies fail.

2 Nostradamus: Seer of the Centuries

Many times in the week I am overtaken by an ecstasy.... Sometimes through the flaming missives brought by the angels of fire..., there come before our exterior senses, even our eyes, predictions of future events or things significant to a future happening.

—NOSTRADAMUS TO HIS SON

Jules Verne anticipated the submarine and Leonardo da Vinci the helicopter. But there was another, more celebrated visionary who predicted not only the submarine and air travel, but also air battles, bombardments, nuclear warfare and fallout... *in the 1500s.* He wrote about wars, revolutions, betrayals, executions and treaties long before they happened—some of them right to the date, others with precise and unmistakable detail.

In his day some thought he was writing gibberish. Others took him for a tool of the devil. Even after some of his remarkable predictions came true,

Michel de Nostredame (Nostradamus)
(1503–1566)

there were still those who believed he was a fraud. More recently, though, he has been called such things as "the man who saw tomorrow" or "the man who saw through time." He is, without doubt, the most illustrious and mysterious of seers.

Born Michel de Nostredame, December 14, 1503,[1] at Saint-Rémy, in Provence, France, he is known by his Latinized name, Nostradamus. He was the eldest of the five sons of Jacques and Reynière de Nostradame, a family of Jewish converts to Christ. At a young age he studied mathematics, Hebrew, Greek, Latin and the "celestial science" of astrology under his grandfather's tutelage. At nineteen he studied medicine at Montpellier under the finest physicians. Taking time out to minister to those afflicted by the plague, Nostradamus completed his doctorate and went on to study under the philosopher Julius-César Scaliger.

Nostradamus practiced medicine throughout his life and became a renowned healer, dispensing unorthodox cures. Although he delivered many from the plague, he was unable to save his wife and children. After their tragic deaths he traveled, studied under the most learned minds of Europe, and became fascinated with alchemy, astrology and white magic.

He settled in Salon in 1547, married a widow of means and together they had six children. He converted the top floor of his home in Salon into a study and observatory, where he diligently wrote his prophecies in four-line verses called quatrains. He compiled these in groups of one hundred called Centuries and they were first published in 1555.

As his prophecies proved more and more accurate, Nostradamus' extraordinary fame traveled far and wide.

More Than a Lucky Guess

What sort of world did Nostradamus live in and what kind of world did he foresee? The sixteenth century had not yet seen the development of the steam engine, the bicycle, the locomotive or the automobile. Yet Nostradamus predicted safe travel "by air, land, sea and wave."[2]

In Nostradamus' day, kings were absolute monarchs who ruled by divine right. In France, where he lived, there were no juries, much less trial by jury for a commoner. To try a monarch was unthinkable. Yet Nostradamus predicted "the queen sent to death by jurors chosen by lot,"[3] which is precisely what happened to Marie Antoinette.

The age of Nostradamus had barely seen the discovery of the New World. Yet the French seer mentions the "government of America" more than two hundred years before the fact. Even fifty years before the American Revolution, few would have guessed that the colonies would rebel against the English Crown, much less defeat what was then the most powerful empire on earth. But, then, Nostradamus did what is humanly impossible.

What would you say are the odds of "guessing" the month and year in which two nations make a treaty—and then naming the two nations, picking the winner, and specifying a major outcome of the event? If there were only fifteen nations in the world in 1555, and there were more, the odds of a lucky guess would be 1 in 11,299,680.[4] Yet Nostradamus was that accurate.

In October of 1727, Persia and Turkey terminated a conflict in which the Turks, who had lost the war, signed a very favorable treaty and won the peace. Some 172 years earlier, Nostradamus described this event in a quatrain which reads:

> The third climate comprehended under Aries,
> The year thousand seven hundred twenty
>   and seven in October,
> The King of Persia taken by those of Egypt,
> Conflict, death, loss, great opprobrium
>   to the cross.[5]   III.77

The quatrain does not mention the Turks, but according to Stewart Robb, an authority on Nostradamus, *those of Egypt* is a synecdoche for the Turks.

A synecdoche is a figure of speech in which a part is used for the whole (or vice versa), such as "Washington, D.C." for the "United States." Egypt had been part of the Ottoman Empire since 1517.

Robb points out that "in 1727, those of Egypt were the Turks," and the extension of their power was "opprobrious to Christianity." Although the Shah was not captured or killed, Robb argues that in consideration of the treaty he signed—in which he dismembered his nation by ceding western Persia to the Turks—the Shah was nevertheless "taken" or conquered.[6]

That was by no means the only time Nostradamus named, against all odds, the date of a future event. In another quatrain he gives the date of the "Seventh War" (around 1580) and the "War of Spanish Succession" (1703).[7] In his prophetic Epistle to Henry II of France, he predicted an event that would be fulfilled with astounding accuracy in 1792, more than two hundred years later.

Prophecies of the French Revolution

In his letter to Henry II, Nostradamus said that "the Christian Church will be persecuted more fiercely than it ever was in Africa, and this will last up to the year 1792, which they will believe to mark a renewal of time."[8]

France was a Catholic country, but in 1792 it was in the midst of the French Revolution and the Church was experiencing just the kind of savage persecution Nostradamus had predicted. The National Convention abolished the monarchy and threw out the Gregorian calendar because of its Christian associations. It introduced its own secular "revolutionary calendar," and proclaimed the first day of "the Year I of the French Republic." This "renewal of time," as Nostradamus put it, took place, as predicted, in 1792.

That little bit of prognostication did not go unnoticed by skeptics ancient or modern. Edgar Leoni says that it is here that Nostradamus was "closest to a bull's-eye." Leoni cites a reference in the February 1792 edition of the *Journal historique et littéraire* to a royalist newspaper, the *Journal de la ville,* that published this particular prophecy and informed readers that the "copy of Nostradamus, in which this prediction is found, will remain exposed in our office for eight days, so that the curious will be able to verify it for themselves."

"The editor of the magazine then goes on to explain," says Leoni, "how, though Nostradamus is generally conceded to be a fraud, he might have been divinely inspired for just this one marvelous prophecy."[9]

Nostradamus' accuracy was not restricted to dates. In fact, few of his predictions have them, although he said in his letter to Henry II that "if I had wanted to date each quatrain, I could have done so."[10] Rather, he couched his prophecies in terms so specific that the circumstances they fit are unmistakably related to one event, historical circumstance or series of related events. The following quatrain illustrates his divine genius:

> The husband, alone, afflicted, will be mitred
> Return, conflict will take place at the Tuileries:
> By five hundred, one betrayer will be titled
> Narbon and Saulce, we have oil with knives.[11]
>
> IX.34

Narbon and Saulce. Two specific names. Suppose Nostradamus had written Simon and Garfunkel, Burns and Allen, or Rodgers and Hammerstein? The mere fact that he had mentioned their names centuries before the fact would have been impressive. Yet here he not only names Narbonne and Sauce (the eighteenth-century forms of Narbon and Saulce) but shows them to be key players in a sociopolitical drama that would ultimately change the course of history.

The French seer was describing one of the great turning points in the French Revolution, a crucial scene in the tragedy of Louis XVI and Marie Antoinette—their ill-fated attempted escape from Paris made on the night of June 20, 1791.

A Death Knell for the Monarchy

Louis XVI and Marie Antoinette were under virtual house arrest at the heavily guarded Tuileries in Paris and their situation was growing ever more desperate. They decided to flee to a point on the border of Luxembourg, where they were to be met by Austrian troops sent by Emperor Leopold II, the queen's brother. Disguised, the king and queen slipped out of Paris and the royal coach made it as far as Varennes, a town near the border.

In Varennes, the king and queen were recognized and then detained. Since their papers were in order, though there was still some question about their identity, Monsieur Sauce, a grocer and the mayor of the town, was at first inclined to let them pass. Under pressure, he had them held in Varennes and invited them into his combination grocery store/ home until their identity could be verified.

Once positively identified, the king tore off his disguise and warmly embraced his captors. Sauce, however, forced them to remain there until word came from the Assembly. He then turned them over to the guard, who brought them back to Paris—and ultimately their doom. This turn of events in the lives of the king and queen sealed their fate and sounded the death knell for the monarchy and the monarchs.

Sauce could twice have saved the king and queen by simply letting them go. Even while held in Sauce's home, Marie Antoinette pleaded with Mme Sauce to release them. "I would like to, Your Highness," she replied, "for I love my king, but I love my husband too and would not have him lose his head." Thus Sauce, as Nostradamus predicted, betrayed the king, who was forced to *"return,"* as the quatrain says, to Paris.

In addition, Sauce sold oil in his grocery shop. The cans were suspended from the rafters and the shop smelled of rancid oil. It seems as if Nostradamus actually recorded a line of dialogue spoken by the proprietor to a customer, more than two hundred years before the fact: *"Sauce, 'we have oil.'"*[12]

Shortly after Louis XVI's return to Paris, Count Narbonne was made Louis' Minister of War. Narbonne was one among the nobility whose actions powerfully contributed to Louis' ruin. We have, therefore, two betrayers: Narbonne, who, as specified in the quatrain, was titled; and Sauce, a bourgeois who was given a 20,000 livre reward by the Assembly for his patriotic act and was showered with praise—and later guillotined.

Once the king and queen were back at the Tuileries, the already ugly mood in Paris drifted rapidly towards the frenzy of violence known as "the reign of terror." On August 10, 1792, a carefully organized mob attacked the Tuileries, set it afire and killed 600 or so of the Swiss Guard. Leading the mob were 513 Marseillais, who are generally called *"the Five Hundred."*[13]

Then, during the siege, precisely as Nostradamus had written, Louis *(husband)* was confronted by the mob *(five hundred)* at the Tuileries *(conflict will take place at the Tuileries)* without his guards *(alone)*. The mob forced him to put on the red cap of liberty used by the revolutionaries *(will be mitred)*.

In short, Nostradamus described with great accuracy a sequence of events in the life of a future king and queen at a turning point in French history, and he did it with an amazing economy of words. In the process he provided such exact detail that it could apply to no other set of historical circumstances.

The "Intolerable Pest"

Although Nostradamus seems to have written a good many predictions about the French Revolution, his interests varied widely. He named and described circumstances in the life of "the heroic [Marshal] de Villars," Louis XIV's ablest and most valiant general; chronicled the rise and fall of Napoleon; named and detailed events in the lives of Franco and Hitler; and described the Bolshevik Revolution some 362 years in advance.[14]

When Nostradamus' prophecies first appeared, they were enthusiastically received by those in the leisure classes who had read the earlier predictions he published in an annual almanac. They were, however, greeted with scorn and derision by a superstitious populace. The less-educated masses took Nostradamus for a tool of the devil.

He was accused of madness, impiety, ignorance of astrology and indiscriminate consumption of alcoholic beverages. He was criticized by physicians, astrologers, philosophers and poets. One taunting critic wrote, "Where do you get that stuff? You intolerable pest, leading people astray with your false teachings full of abomination."[15]

When some of his prophecies came true, however, Catherine de' Medici, wife of Henry II, invited Nostradamus to court, where he found favor. Yet when he published several more Centuries in 1558, his adversaries grew in number. Some even demanded that he be arraigned before the Holy Inquisition.

A Fatal Joust

In 1559, Nostradamus' fame became assured when Henry II died after a jousting accident on July 10, in exactly the manner Nostradamus had predicted in quatrain 35 of the first Century.

The quatrain reads in part, "The young lion [Count de Montgomery, Captain of the Scottish Guard] will overcome the old one [Henry II] / On the field of battle in single combat: / He will put out his eyes in a 'cage of gold,'" taken to mean the king's gilded helmet. With an apparent medical diagnosis of his injury, "two fractures one," the predicted outcome was that Henry II would "die a cruel death."[16]

The fatal tournament was to celebrate the double wedding of Henry's sister Elisabeth to Philip II of Spain, and his daughter Marguerite to Emmanuel Philibert, Duke of Savoy. The tournament lasted for three days. Henry acquitted himself admirably in the lists and asked Gabriel Montgomery to ride against him in the last course of the day. He declined but Henry commanded him to obey.

Catherine pleaded with Henry not to participate in the joust. In his biography of the queen, Jean Héritier reports that Catherine "had expected for a long time that her husband would die a violent death. The *Centuries* of Nostradamus...had predicted such a death for him. The Queen was obsessed by the fatal quatrain."

Héritier goes on to say that "Nostradamus' prediction coincided exactly with that of Lucca Gaurico. The Italian bishop-astrologer, who was world-famous, approved by the Popes—by Julius II and Leo X as well as Clement VII and Paul III—had told Henri II, three years before Nostradamus published his Centuries, to avoid all single combat, especially in his forties, as at that period of his life he would be in danger of a head wound which might lead to blindness or death.... [Catherine] begged the King in vain not to take part in the tournament."[17]

Henry liked tournaments, ignored the prophecy and, as a result of a freak accident, was pierced in or above the eye by a splinter of Montgomery's broken lance which slipped under his visor. The king died a *cruel death* ten days later. Word of Nostradamus' prophecy and Henry's death spread to all corners of Europe, and the French seer's fame never wavered thereafter. Ever since, Nostradamus has been praised by some and vilified by others.

Enigmatic Sentences and Exacting Prophecies

In a preface to his prophecies, written to his infant son, Nostradamus claims that his visions reached to the year 3797—a place few of us have ever visited in our wildest imagination. It is Nostradamus' prophecies for our time that become the most fascinating—and frightening. With no less foresight and perspicacity than he demonstrated while penning the history of future events that have now passed us by, Nostradamus has left us a vivid description of the challenges our generation may soon face.

Let us bear in mind as we consider them that Nostradamus said his predictions were divinely inspired and supported by astrological calculation. I believe that the spirit of prophecy that was upon Nostradamus came through the heart of Saint Germain. Nostradamus himself described the setting in which he received his prophecies.

Nostradamus is alone at night, seated in his secret study, which he tells us is a specially built room in his attic, when "a small flame comes out of the solitude and brings things to pass which should not be thought vain."[18] Then, when all is set: "Divine splendor. The divine seats himself nearby."[19] In this description, taken from the opening quatrains of Century I, the prophet suggests that he enters a meditative state and like an amanuensis records what "the divine" tells him.

It is often argued that Nostradamus' prophecies are so vague that they can be applied to virtually anything. "The style of the Centuries is so multiform and nebulous," wrote historian Jean Gimon, summarizing this line of criticism, "that each may, with a little effort and good will, find in them what he seeks."[20] That is not actually the case. Nostradamus intended his "enigmatic sentences," as he explained to Henry II, to have "only one sense and meaning, and nothing ambiguous or amphibological [capable of having more than one interpretation] inserted."[21]

Nostradamus' prophecies, therefore, are obscure until overtaken by events. When the events occur, the quatrains become eminently clear and, because of his precise use of language, allow only one possible interpretation for each quatrain or series of related quatrains.

The "Narbon and Saulce" quatrain, as we saw, can scarcely apply to anything other than the tragedy that befell Louis XVI in the eighteenth century. In another quatrain Nostradamus stipulates that certain events will occur "in the year that France has a one-eyed king,"[22] which, as we have seen by the ten days the wounded Henry II ruled France, was 1559. No other one-eyed king has ever held the French throne; hence that is the only possible year for the prophecy. The quatrain predicting the treaty of October 1727 between the Persians and Turks is also extremely exacting.

Disguised Prophecies

While Nostradamus described future events in concrete terms that limited his predictions to specific situations, the language he used added a mystical dimension to his prophecies. This mystical language helps convey his meaning and intent and reveals the depth and breadth of his own perceptions.

Nostradamus' prophecies were obscure by design. The reasons for this are as complex as the quatrains themselves. He was writing at a time when one accused of witchcraft or black magic could be burned at the stake. Lee McCann, author of *Nostradamus: The Man Who Saw Through Time,* reminds us that "while Nostradamus was a boy preparing [to continue his education at] Avignon, five hundred of the piteous creatures accused of witchcraft were burned in Geneva."[23]

Nostradamus did not want to be summarily executed by potential adversaries in Church or State. Nor did he want to interfere with God's will by prematurely revealing the prophecies he was given. Nostradamus therefore set his prophecies down in a deliberately hard-to-understand mystical prose. In order to further disguise them he rewrote them into cryptic quatrains in chronologically organized Centuries.

The quatrains contain a bewildering mixture of

French, Latin, Greek, Italian, Provençal, symbols, astrological configurations, anagrams, synecdoches, puns and other literary devices. Still he thought they were too easy. Nostradamus mentions a number of times that he is concerned about "the danger of the times" and "the calumny of evil men." Just to be sure, he scrambled the order prior to their publication in 1555.[24]

In 1564, Nostradamus reached the summit of his career. While on a tour through France, the young King Charles IX and his mother, Queen Catherine de' Medici, visited the prophet. The queen titled him Counselor and Physician in Ordinary. Not long after, in 1566, Nostradamus died in his study. He had left unfinished the seventh of his ten centuries and had barely begun an eleventh and a twelfth.

His epitaph read in part: "Here rests the bones of the illustrious Michel Nostradamus, alone of all mortals judged worthy to record with his almost divine pen, under the influence of the stars, the future events of the entire world."

3 A Time of Peace or a Time of War?

We are quick to flare up,
we races of men on the earth.
—HOMER

Nostradamus himself tells us that his prophecies, written in code, are enigmatic and obscure—until the time of their fulfillment. This has led to differences of opinion among the best and most popular of Nostradamus' commentators about what we can expect for the near and distant future.

Nevertheless, many interpreters of Nostradamus say that several of his quatrains deal with war, plague and even nuclear catastrophes. At the same time, our mysterious seer of the centuries describes windows of peace and a golden age to come. This chapter covers some of Nostradamus' most notable quatrains on war and peace.

Some of Nostradamus' prophecies are intense. By exploring their meaning, I am in no way assuming that they will come to pass. I don't take a doomsday approach or a millennialist stance. I am writing this book because I believe that every one of us *can* do something to turn back the negatives.

Prophecy is not set in stone. It is my constant prayer that the spiritual people of earth, aware of the worst-case scenarios and the karmic factors that underlie them, will rally and take up the spiritual techniques that can turn the future into a best-case scenario. And I'm hoping, with Carl Sandburg, that "sometime they'll give a war and nobody will come."

Metaphors for Our Time

When contemplating Nostradamus' quatrains, remember that he purposely held back elements of what he knew because, he said, "some given to censure would raise difficulties."[1] Furthermore, Nostradamus was describing technologies and effects that those of his age could scarcely imagine, and therefore he had to resort to metaphor.

Just think how challenging it would be for someone in the sixteenth century to describe an airplane, the blast of a nuclear warhead or a satellite circling the earth. Yet things that were unfamiliar to readers in Nostradamus' time become amazingly clear in ours. Take Century II, quatrain 91:

> At sunrise one will see a great fire,
> Noise and light extending towards Aquilon:
> Within the circle death and one will hear cries,
> Through steel, fire, famine, death awaiting
>   them.[2]   II.91

Note the vivid description, economy of words and adept use of language with which Nostradamus paints his scene. Death *through steel* (also translated as "weapons"), *fire* and eventually *famine* is an accurate description of what could take place *within the circle,* or blast radius of a nuclear warhead. *Aquilon* means "North," a name interpreters of Nostradamus take to stand for Russia and sometimes the United States, but in general the nations of the "north."

I see a mystical way of interpreting this quatrain as well. First, *sunrise* can be seen as the time of the rising of the "Sun of Righteousness," the Christ consciousness within one or the few or the many. The ancients taught that at the apocalyptic moment of a great enlightenment or the appearance of a Cosmic Christ, there is fire, noise and light. The descent of light is for the purging of darkness to make way for a greater assimilation of God's light.

In addition, the French word *glaive* in this quatrain, which some translate as "steel" or "weapons," means literally a "two-edged sword." Since this term is used in the Book of Revelation to describe one like the "Son of man" out of whose mouth comes a "sharp two-edged sword,"[3] this quatrain may imply a kind of judgment.

The imagery of the next quatrain is likewise intense and fearsome:

> There will be unleashed live fire, hidden death,
> Horrible and frightful within the globes,
> By night the city reduced to dust by the fleet,
> The city afire, the enemy amenable.[4]   V.8

While commentators say this quatrain could fit the U.S. attack on Hiroshima and Nagasaki in 1945 or even other bombings during World War II (*globes* could be an apt description of bombs), they do not rule out the possibility that it prophesies a devastation the world has not yet witnessed.

"Fighting in the Sky"

In the 1500s, the picture that emerges from the next quatrain must have seemed like the vision of someone in a delirium. Today it takes on the eerie quality of a nuclear blast and air battles that some strange-looking creatures take part in:

They will think they have seen the Sun at night
When they will see the pig half-man:
Noise, song, battle, fighting in the sky perceived,
And one will hear brute beasts talking.[5]   I.64

In our time, *noise, song, battle, fighting in the sky perceived* is all too easy to imagine. The brilliance of the *Sun at night* gives the sense of a nuclear event. Perhaps, since the word *Sun* is capitalized, an apocalyptic character is intended.

It is nothing less than astonishing that in using the phrase *they will think they have seen the Sun at night,* Nostradamus has closely paraphrased the actual words of the first civilians to unknowingly witness an atomic explosion.

Three weeks before an atomic bomb was dropped on Hiroshima, the world's first atomic bomb was detonated in a predawn test in the desert at Alamogordo, New Mexico. Mrs. H. E. Weiselman, 150 miles away on the Arizona/New Mexico state line, witnessed the flash, which she said "was just like the sun had come up and then suddenly gone down again."[6]

Then, in March of 1954, twenty-three Japanese fishermen aboard the Lucky Dragon Number Five inadvertently sailed into the testing area around Bikini Atoll in the central Pacific. They were 100 miles from the island when a nuclear test was conducted.

The fishermen said the blast looked like a "second sun rising in the west early in the morning."[7]

What about *the pig half-man*? This image has puzzled commentators for some time. Erika Cheetham, author of a number of books on Nostradamus, says this phrase "seems a clear picture of a pilot in silhouette wearing an oxygen mask, helmet and goggles. The oxygen breathing apparatus does look remarkably like a pig's snout. The battle is clearly described as being fought in the air; the screams may be the sound of dropping bombs as they whine to earth. The battle is clearly watched... by people on the ground.

"It is important to understand the wording of the last line. The aeroplanes, 'bestes brutes,' are heard talking to others. Could this be a forecast of radio communication? Certainly this quatrain helps to convince me that Nostradamus' visions were of two dimensions, both visual and aural."[8]

The prophet is not only clairvoyant but clairaudient, capable of reading the future, not necessarily as a handwriting on the wall but as a videotape projected on a screen.

War, Pestilence and Fire

Another quatrain describing war and possibly nuclear conflict is:

The horrible war which is being prepared
   in the West,
The following year will come the pestilence
So very horrible that young, old, nor beast,
Blood, fire Mercury, Mars, Jupiter in France.[9]

IX.55

Commentators have related this quatrain to the outbreak of influenza following World War I. Yet some modern interpreters see the words *pestilence* and *blood* as a possible reference to two current blood-related diseases—AIDS and the sickness caused by the Ebola virus—or the devastation that would be caused by chemical or biological warfare.[10]

"The Sky Will Burn"

Another encoded reading of the signs of our times seems to describe nuclear war or a nuclear incident:

At forty-five degrees the sky will burn,
Fire to approach the great new city:
In an instant a great scattered flame
   will leap up,
When one will want to demand proof
   of the Normans.[11]   VI.97

What is the identity of the *great new city?* Commentators have made several proposals, including

Geneva, Paris, New York, Villeneuve-sur-Lot in France and even the Vatican.

Erika Cheetham believes "the advent of the Third World War, according to Nostradamus, will be heralded by an attack upon New York—city and state—through both bombs and chemical warfare." Persuaded, as other commentators are, that the events described by this quatrain take place along the 45th parallel, she says, "The state of New York lies between the 40th and 45th parallel in the U.S.A.... The attack appears to be very widespread, covering both the state and the new city, and the scattered flame may well be that of a nuclear holocaust."[12]

Nostradamus may not be talking about a degree of latitude here. As I contemplate Nostradamus meditating on revelations given him by his divine source, I see him noting his visions in code as a chronicler of events, a journalist getting the scoop on the future. And Nostradamus "sees" from various vantage points. Thus another possible interpretation for this quatrain is that in his "session" Nostradamus is standing atop a high tower in the new city observing the 45-degree angle of elevation of a nuclear airburst from a warhead aimed at the city.

While this assessment is a departure from other interpreters, neither the original French nor the

English translation says "45th parallel" or "latitude" (although many seem to have taken wide latitude in their interpretations).

From what we have been able to glean from the United States Air Force, North American Air Defense Command (NORAD) and several military planners, the 45-degree-angle theory is certainly worth considering. Forty-five degrees could be an angle of approach for a warhead, although such angles, the experts say, would vary considerably depending on where it was fired and the purpose of the attack.

The precise angle at which warheads would approach a major city like New York is classified information. According to one knowledgeable source, although warheads from ICBMs are more likely to come in at an angle of about 65 or 70 degrees, warheads carried by a missile fired from the deck of a ship at relatively close range would be more likely to come in at 45 degrees. Nevertheless, at any angle of entry, it is still possible to observe the *sky burn*.

Nostradamus' quatrains that seem to allude to nuclear incidents don't necessarily portend war. In today's world, they may much better describe nuclear accidents or even nuclear terrorism. In addition to the Big Five of the nuclear club (Russia, the

United States, Britain, France and China), India and Pakistan have shown that they can make and explode nuclear weapons. Israel is known to have nuclear capability. North Korea, Iran and possibly Libya are believed to be developing nuclear warheads.

In addition, both the United States and Russia acknowledge that the Y2K problem heightens the possibility of being spooked into an accidental nuclear launch. Russian officials have even appealed to the U.S. Defense Department and NATO to help update the computers that control the Russian nuclear arsenal. Commenting on the Y2K problem, Pentagon spokesperson Susan Hansen has said, "None of us knows exactly what's going to happen."[13]

A Spiritual Interpretation

On an entirely different track, I would not rule out a spiritual interpretation of Century VI, quatrain 97. Spiritually speaking, *the sky will burn, fire* and *flame* could all indicate a celestial phenomenon that might have spiritual import, or even an aurora borealis.

What of *proof of the Normans*? *Normans* literally means "men of the north." If you were to write in code, you might describe the heaven-world as "north" and its inhabitants as "men of the north"— that is, the angels, masters and saints who reach out to us spiritually from the heaven-world. Perhaps we will be turning to these enlightened ones at the time of the fulfillment of this prophecy to understand the spiritual significance of what is taking place.

"Very Great Famine"

Nostradamus has also described a time of famine. Some speculate that these trials may be the result of a bacteriological attack or fallout.

> The great famine that I sense approaching,
> Often turning, then to be universal,
> So great and long that one will tear
> The root from the wood and the child
>   from the breast.[14]   I.67

> Very great famine by pestiferous wave,
> By long rain the length of the Arctic pole:
> Samarobryn hundred leagues from the
>   hemisphere,
> They will live without law exempt
>   from politics.[15]   VI.5

The key word in the last quatrain is *pestiferous,* which means "carrying or propagating infectious disease" or "infected with a pestilential disease." Thus, the first two lines of the quatrain could describe a *very great famine* caused by a *wave* carrying a deadly disease or nuclear contamination that traverses the Arctic pole. It obviously reaches a populated area (because it causes a *great famine*).

Of even greater interest is the mysterious term *samarobryn,* which continues to puzzle students of Nostradamus. Since "hundred leagues" is 270 miles, some suggest that *samarobryn* may refer to a satellite or space station. Edgar Leoni, for instance, says, "Might we not here have a prophecy of a space-station thought by Nostradamus, rightly or wrongly, to be about 270 miles from the earthly hemisphere?" He also ventures a wild guess that *samarobryn* might be Nostradamus' attempt at writing down the unfamiliar name of someone associated with this future space venture, a name like Sam R. O'Brien.[16]

Cheetham suggests that *samarobryn* is derived from the Russian words *samo* (self) and *robin* (operator) and therefore refers to "a self-operating machine in space."[17] Rene Noorbergen offers another intriguing idea. He says that Nostradamus may have used the Latin words *samara* (a seed pod with one or two wings) and a form of the verb *obire* (to wander, travel, encircle) to describe a spherical object circling the earth at an altitude of 270 miles. "In modern terms," Noorbergen says, "this is very probably a satellite or space platform with one or two solar panels."[18]

Cheetham also says that *samarobryn* may be a word formed from Suramin and Ribavrin, two of the drugs that have been used to treat the *pestiferous wave* of AIDS. "Perhaps the remedy for AIDS," she wonders, "will be produced in a sterile laboratory circling the earth?"[19] As John Hogue points out, "In the summer of 1992 one U.S. space shuttle mission experimented with proteins in zero gravity to find a cure for AIDS.... The cryptic double-talk of the final line [of Nostradamus' quatrain] that exempts those flying in space from law and politics may be positive in nature. To save our world from diseases the scientists in zero-gravity labs are working beyond the petty concerns of nationalism and politics."[20]

Stewart Robb takes the word *samarobryn* to stand for "Sam Rayburn," the U.S.S. *Sam Rayburn,* that is—a missile-carrying submarine. Nostradamus "may have intended instead a submarine station from which is shot a missile with a trajectory of 270 miles or so from the hemisphere," says Robb. "To check, I phoned Rockwell International, in Fullerton, and learned indeed from a good authority that though 270 miles is rather high, the missile could indeed push that far up and no doubt sometimes would."[21]

Given this line of reasoning, it's surprising that no one has yet suggested that *samarobryn* may have something to do with surface-to-air missiles, otherwise known as SAMs.

The Shrinking World

In Century I, quatrain 63, Nostradamus fore-
sees a period of peace in a shrinking world, followed by wars:

The scourges passed the world shrinks,
For a long time peace and populated lands:
One will travel safely by air, land, sea and wave,
Then the wars stirred up anew.[22]   I.63

The key to interpreting this quatrain is the French
word *fléaux,* meaning "scourges." A scourge is "a
whip that is used to inflict pain or punishment," or
"a cause of widespread affliction"—which could
also describe what happens when negative karma
descends upon the unprepared. The word *fléaux*
also means "plagues," which can be defined as "an
epidemic disease causing a high rate of mortality"
or "a disastrous evil or affliction." Today such a
plague, or *scourge,* could take many forms, from an
epidemic to a war to sickness resulting from nuclear
radiation.

"The most interesting aspect of this quatrain,"
says Cheetham, "is the manner in which Nostradamus grasps the very twentieth-century concept
that air travel makes the whole world accessible—it
'becomes smaller.' It is worth noting that the so-called
era of world peace since 1945 is the longest unbroken

one this century. But it could soon be broken if we are to believe Nostradamus. The extinguished pestilence [i.e., *scourges passed*] may refer to disease or the after-effects of the Second World War."[23]

A Golden Age Dawns

While Nostradamus certainly seems to point to periods of war, famine and affliction, he also speaks of a time of peace. In his Epistle to King Henry II of France, Nostradamus first describes a time of such degradation that much of the world will see war. Cities and buildings will be destroyed, women raped, children dashed and broken against town walls.

So many evils will be committed, says the prophet, that "nearly all the world will find itself undone and desolated." Before these events, rare birds will cry, "Today, today," and then "sometime later will vanish." After this, the seer predicts, "there will be almost renewed another reign of Saturn and a golden age." Saturn is the Roman god who ruled a golden age, and his reign is often interpreted to be the age of Aquarius.

"Hearing the affliction of his people," Nostradamus continues, God will command "Satan" (a possible symbol for evil or the dark side of humanity) to be cast into the bottomless pit and bound for a thousand years. "Then a universal peace will commence between God and man" until "Satan" is again unbound.[24]

In an intriguing interpretation, John Hogue says that Nostradamus used animal riddles and that the birds he mentions may symbolize "the religious visionary who will help to stave off the dire events described." Hogue says, "The key to avert disaster may come from dropping the outmoded past and turning away from obsessions with a tomorrow that never comes. Humanity must gather its genius, energy, and love and pour it onto the present."[25]

Peace, Union and Change

Nostradamus again speaks of a time of peace in these two quatrains:

> There will be peace, union and change,
> Estates, offices, low high and high very low:
> To prepare a trip, the first offspring torment,
> War to cease, civil process, debates.[26]   IX.66

> Mars and the scepter [i.e., Jupiter] will be
>   found conjoined
> Under Cancer calamitous war:
> Shortly afterwards a new King will be
>   anointed,
> One who for a long time will pacify the earth.[27]
>   VI.24

The next time *Mars* and *Jupiter* are conjoined (are at or near the same degree in the heavens) is June 21, 2002, or early April 2002.[28] "For the first time in the quatrains," says Cheetham, "Nostradamus allows that a period of peace may follow the war. If Wölner's dating of the conjunction is correct [June 21, 2002], there is a future for the world after the Millennium."[29]

John Hogue adds, however, that Nostradamus also provides an implicit warning. "Nostradamus... predicts a millennium of peace and wisdom, but his insights also take him further," writes Hogue. "He is able to look past this era and warns us that this Aquarian humanity, although achieving an equilibrium between the opposites of science and religion, could easily turn in on itself and become selfish....

"From Nostradamus' *Epistle to King Henry II* we can interpret that, by the dawn of the Fourth Millennium after Christ, even the power of Satan could be unleashed by our inability to maintain awareness of ourselves and our essence."[30]

Thus, mankind will always have the choice and the challenge to express its highest self or fall prey to its darker desires.

As I said in chapter 1, the new millennium brings with it this same choice. It brings the winds of freedom and progress as well as the possibility of finding new solutions to problems. We are compelled to change and grow, but we must trim our sails and set our course so that the winds of freedom do not carry us into unbridled revolution or anarchy.

What will we use our new freedom to achieve? Will we harness it wisely to liberate the finest part of ourselves and to create a better world, or will we use it to carry out the agenda of the ego without regard for the greater community of which we are all a part? Will we create a time of peace or a time of war?

4 A Parable for Our Time

The gods love the obscure and hate the obvious.
                    —THE UPANISHADS

Nostradamus made hundreds, perhaps thousands of predictions. He said that his prophecies reached beyond the year 3000—until 3797, to be exact. Yet he singled out only a few exact dates when those prophecies would be fulfilled. One of them is a date on the very cusp of the new millennium: "the year 1999, seventh month."

Those words open what is perhaps the most celebrated of Nostradamus' quatrains. It is also one of the most enigmatic. As the extraordinary seer tells us in the preface to his Centuries, he purposely tried to render his prophecies "a bit obscurely."

The famous quatrain reads:

> The year 1999, seventh month,
> From the sky will come a great King of Terror:
> To bring back to life the great
>   King of Angolmois,
> Before and after Mars to reign by good luck.[1]
>
> X. 72

Does this quatrain suggest an invasion, a missile attack or an attack by unknown forces? Does it predict that the earth will be hit by an asteroid or comet? Hollywood has certainly dramatized that scenario with movies like *Armageddon* and *Deep Impact*. Or does this prophecy have a less ominous and even noble meaning?

Like many other quatrains of Nostradamus, this one must be approached as if it were a Zen koan. For what seems obvious may not be obvious at all. The most intriguing element of this quatrain, though, is that it not only relates to "1999," but to how we must treat the whole subject of prophecy and our future. It is a parable for our time.

"The Seventh Month"

Even the exact date of Nostradamus' prediction is controversial. Many commentators assume that the *seventh month* means July. What Nostradamus actually wrote was *sept mois*, which in French can mean "seven month" or "seven months." Therefore another possibility is that Nostradamus meant seven months into 1999, which would be the end of July or the beginning of August.

Furthermore, Nostradamus may have been using the Julian calendar, which is thirteen days earlier than the Gregorian calendar currently in use. If that is the case, Nostradamus' vision of "July" could be anywhere from July 14 through August 13 in our current reckoning of time. Some interpreters even postulate that the *seventh month* refers to September, which in Latin literally means "seventh month."[2]

A Great King of Terror

The date is only the first of the conundrums surrounding this quatrain. Even more pivotal—and perplexing—is its cast of characters, starting with the *great King of Terror*.

Several interpreters of Nostradamus say the *King of Terror* that comes *from the sky* could be anything from a warlord to a warhead to a free-falling asteroid. With what we (don't) know about Y2K and its computer glitches, it's not out of the question that the *terror* could be the result of some unforeseen military computer problem triggering a false alarm and a missile attack.

Terror, as in *terrorism,* is a word we've been hearing a lot these days. Thus, it is also possible that Nostradamus' *King of Terror* has something to do with the growing threat of terrorism. When it comes to terrorism in this day and age, our imaginations aren't limited to explosives. The *terror* from the *sky* may be closer to a bioterrorist attack where a cloud of anthrax spores silently claims millions of lives within two to three days. At least ten nations, including Iraq, have worked to develop anthrax as a warfare agent.

There has even been talk that Iraq's Saddam Hussein is reaching out to the Saudi exile Osama bin Laden, who is calling for Muslims to wage a holy war against Americans and all "enemies of Islam." As *Newsweek* put it, if these two enemies of America join forces, "it would be a marriage made in hell."[3]

Not everyone, however, sees Nostradamus' *King* as ominous. For instance, author and translator Peter Lemesurier claims that the French in this quatrain which most translate as *of terror (d'effraieur)* is possibly a misprint for *desfraieur,* from the Old French meaning "to defray, settle, pay up." This is plausible since in Nostradamus' day the letters *f* and *s* looked very much alike: *f∫*.

If Lemesurier's guess is correct, then instead

of *King of Terror* the phrase would read *King who defrays* or, as Lemesurier translates it, "a great financing lord." In other words, Nostradamus may be talking about a magnate with megabucks who travels by airplane *(from the sky)* to finance *(bring back to life)* some cause.[4]

A King of the Mongols or a Renaissance King?

The *King of Terror* or the *King who defrays*, says Nostradamus, will bring back to life the *King of Angolmois*. The problem is, nobody really knows what *Angolmois* is. Most commentators say *Angolmois* is an anagram for *Mongoulois,* or Mongolian. An anagram is a word created by transposing the letters of another word. There is no *a* in *Mongoulois* (which is needed to create *Mongoulois* from *Angolmois*), yet most commentators still interpret the *King of Angolmois* as "King of the Mongols."

If Nostradamus did mean "King of the Mongols," then his quatrain could be telling us that the *King of Terror* will *bring back to life* a vast destruction and bloody genocide like the one wrought by the Mongol king Genghis Khan. This may be correct—or it may be a very big assumption.

Here's a new possibility that's at least as plausible and that extracts an entirely new meaning from this quatrain. There is a region in France called

Angoumois, which is only one letter off from Nostradamus' *Angolmois*. Commentators have discarded this association, drawing a blank on just who the King of Angoumois might be.

Yet it is entirely possible that Nostradamus was referring to a well-known and beloved French king: Francis I of France, known as François d'Angoulême—the capital of Angoumois. What makes this interpretation so compelling is that Francis I reigned during Nostradamus' own lifetime.

Francis I was the first of five monarchs of the Angoulême branch of the House of Valois. He fought a number of wars with the Holy Roman Empire, but he went down in French history as a patron of the arts and a knightly king—a Renaissance ruler. Leonardo da Vinci was among those he generously sponsored.

This popular and intelligent king filled his court with poets, musicians and scholars, promoted chivalry and gallantry, and spent money lavishly, quite like a *king who defrays* in fact. He traveled throughout France on horseback to learn about his land and meet his countrymen face to face. He graciously emptied prisons and treated his people with warmth and largesse.

If Nostradamus was in fact alluding to a king like Francis I, then perhaps the intended meaning of the quatrain is *from the sky will come a great king who defrays* to bring back to life the great King of Angoumois, Francis I. In other words, the quatrain may suggest that a mogul of some sort or a social group with considerable resources, financial or spiritual, will sponsor the kind of renaissance that Francis I kindled during Nostradamus' own lifetime.

A Chinese Puzzle

Another intriguing, although less likely, interpretation for the *King* who comes *from the sky* has to do with NASA's *Cassini* spacecraft, scheduled to fly by Earth in August of 1999 on its way to Saturn.

This interpretation, offered by Goro Adachi,[5] uses the alternate translation *King who defrays* (that is, one who pays or bears the expense of something). This "rich" king, he says, could be a symbolic allusion to Saturn, who in Roman mythology was both a god of agriculture and a ruler of a past golden age. Thus, *from the sky will come a great King who defrays* (Saturn) may refer to the August flyby of NASA's Saturn probe.

This probe is carrying seventy-two pounds of deadly plutonium dioxide fuel and could turn into a *King of Terror* if somehow it exploded as it flew by the earth. Such a scenario worries anti-nuclear activists, even though NASA says the chance that the *Cassini* spacecraft would hit the earth is less than one in a million. Of course, any space probe or even the space station *Mir* (originally scheduled to be retired and to crash into the ocean during the summer of 1999) could be a *terror* coming *from the sky* if it accidentally, or as a result of Y2K problems, went into a free fall.

Another interesting correlation is that Mars, mentioned later in this quatrain, has two moons—Phobos ("fear") and Deimos ("terror"). Maybe the *King of Terror* is somehow a reference to Mars itself as the overlord *(King)* of Deimos *(terror)*. Not only is Mars a possible candidate for the *King of Terror*, but in ancient lore Mars is known as the god of war, which ties right back into the warlike King of the Mongols.

The permutations are endless for those who have an imagination.

Although the symbolic connections of interpretations like these sound like a Chinese puzzle, remember that Nostradamus purposely disguised his quatrains and used mystical glyphs to convey the real meaning of his prophecies.

Father of Terrors

Nostradamus' *King of Terror* has yet another possible persona. Approached from an entirely different angle, this quatrain has a potentially enlightening meaning. In the tradition of the Arabs, there is a *Father of Terrors*—the Great Sphinx. The Sphinx has long been thought to be a repository of secret wisdom. It's also right smack in the middle of a controversy.

In his prophetic readings, the seer Edgar Cayce revealed that records of the lost civilization of Atlantis were stored in a "Hall of Records" between the paws of the Great Sphinx. Cayce said these records describe the development of the people on Atlantis and the earth changes that took place on that continent. In 1941, Cayce predicted that in a few years from that time this "tomb of records" would be opened.

Recent testing with seismographs has shown that there are indeed unexplored tunnels and cavities beneath the Sphinx and a large rectangular chamber beneath its paws. This chamber has been linked to the legendary Atlantean Hall of Records. The Egyptian government, however, has not yet allowed anyone to actually search for these underground chambers, but negotiations are continuing.

Some of Nostradamus' commentators say that if the *King of Terror* is a reference to the Egyptian *Father of Terrors,* this quatrain may prophesy in some way the opening of the secret records of Atlantis. How the *Father of Terrors* would come *from the sky* is not clear.

"Mars to Reign by Good Luck"

Mars in the last line of the quatrain is typically associated with anger, war or violence. In astrological parlance, it is also the planet that represents the energy to get things done and action based on desire. As a student of astrology, Nostradamus may have known that Mars was originally a god of agriculture, fertility and the spring. Mars guarded the fields of the people —their abundance and their way of making a living.

"A consideration of the occult meaning of this planet," says John Hogue, "opens up the possibility of a positive outcome in the future. The phrase *before and after Mars rules happily* can be interpreted to mean that the higher aspect of Mars, as the god of magic and spiritual transformation, *rules happily* in the new millennium."[6]

In fact, if you wed this energetic and fruitful meaning of *Mars' reign* to a *defraying king* (rather than a King of Terror) *who brings back to life the great King of Angoumois* (rather than the King of the Mongols), you again get the picture of a rich, make-it-happen philanthropist who ushers in some kind of a transforming renaissance.

Two Meanings, Two Potentials

The fact that there are two ways of understanding Mars, as a god of agriculture or a god of war, reinforces what we have seen throughout this quatrain and what we will see throughout this book—that there are always two ways of approaching every prophecy.

This intricate analysis shows us that the greatly feared Century X, quatrain 72 is not as clear cut as many think. Everything has a double meaning: The *King* could signify a host of terrifying scenarios or he could signify a positive outcome, such as the material or spiritual largesse of a philanthropist or the opening of the secrets of the Great Sphinx. The *King of Angolmois* could be someone like the dreaded King of the Mongols or a figure like the magnanimous Francis I. *Mars' reign* could be warlike or it could be energetic, action-oriented and transformational.

Perhaps both potentials exist—the very good and the very bad—and what finally happens depends on us. That's why this quatrain is a parable for our time. In a symbolic sort of way it tells us that when prophecy is before us, we always have two choices. We can either take the high road (turn the challenge into an opportunity) or we can take the low road (bury our heads in the sand and do nothing).

Nostradamus' quatrain may indeed have serious implications. In the face of any prophecy, it's essential to be aware of the negatives, to understand why they may take place, and to be prepared. But it's also essential to do our spiritual work to overcome the challenges.

If enough people believe in something, they can make it happen as their collective energies come together to fill in their shared vision. The same holds true for the way we deal with prophecy.

As we do our spiritual work, it is paramount that we focus on the desired outcome. Rather than fixate on the negatives and thereby give them power, we must hold the highest vision of good and pool our energies to work toward that goal. We are the prophets of our own destiny. We together can create our own prophecies and we together can make them come true.

Astrological Harbingers

We don't yet know what Nostradamus was seeing as he recorded the famous quatrain 72 of Century X. And it is possible that its meaning will not become evident until months after its fulfillment. Trigger points are sometimes only discovered in retrospect by following the trail of their effects. However, we do know that the astrological configurations for the time frame of this quatrain are daunting.

In the preface to his Centuries, Nostradamus

emphasized that the wise interpretation of astrology can be used to accurately predict future events. "Things which are to happen," he said, "can be prophesied by the lights of the sky at night, which are natural, coupled with the spirit of prophecy."[7]

As I said earlier, astrology can be used to anticipate cycles of returning karma, both good and bad. It's another way of getting a sneak preview of the challenges and opportunities that are open to us. But astrology doesn't tell us precisely what will happen or how we will react to coming events. That's up to us.

In the spirit of Nostradamus, it is worthwhile deciphering what the handwriting in the sky can tell us about our transition into the new millennium— because the year 1999 will have come and gone, but the effects of the astrological events that took place that year will live on.

Astrological configurations sometimes set in motion circumstances that are not fully outplayed for months or even years. Sometimes a future configuration can activate the release of energies that have been quiescent for a period of time.

In addition, if the energies of more than one major configuration begin to interact, the interplay of forces may not give us either the best-case or worst-case scenario, but something in-between. On occasion, the admixture may give us both at the same time.

Rules of Thumb

As we review the following astrological configurations for the second half of 1999, there are three rules of thumb to keep in mind. First, as I said, major transits and configurations initiate momentous cycles of change whose effects can be felt far into the future.

Second, it is best to think of astrological aspects as circuits of energy rather than as good or bad omens. A so-called hard aspect, like a square, is not necessarily a "bad" aspect. Something that is challenging can also be energizing or event-producing. When we look at our challenges as opportunities to gain new ground, there is no such thing as "bad" astrology.

Third, I believe God has given us the understanding of the science of astrology along with accelerated spiritual techniques so that we can chart our returning karma and transmute the negatives before they happen. Keeping this in mind, let's examine just what the handwriting in the skies can tell us about our future opportunities and challenges.

A Hot Spot for Nuclear Energy

In June and July of 1999, transiting Pluto is in a danger zone vis-à-vis the Antares-Aldebaran axis—the hot spot for nuclear energy.

Let me give you some background. Aldebaran,

at 9 degrees Gemini, and Antares, at 9 degrees Sagittarius, are two of the most powerful fixed stars in the heavens. Fixed stars have positive and negative influences. On the positive side, both Aldebaran and Antares are associated with courage, honor, intelligence and the potential for gaining power and wealth. On the negative side, both of them, particularly Antares, are associated with war, sudden destruction, self-destruction, fires, racial and religious intolerance, and nuclear events.

The 8th and 9th degrees of Gemini and Sagittarius are very important in the astrological charts of the first controlled atomic reaction, the first nuclear test and the first use of a nuclear weapon on Hiroshima. Thus, these three atomic incidents make those degrees of the zodiac planetary hot spots.

When planets aspect those degrees, they tend to trigger the kinds of events that have taken place there before. In other words, any major astrological events that aspect 8 or 9 degrees Gemini-Sagittarius have the potential to trigger a nuclear event. In addition, the U.S. conceptional Uranus,[8] at 8 degrees Gemini, falls right on the Antares-Aldebaran axis.

So we have the U.S. conceptional Uranus (the planet of sudden and explosive events) sitting on a planetary axis of two stars related to terrorism, destruction and war. And this same axis is the planetary hot spot for nuclear-weapons use. Also, Uranus rules uranium, an element used in nuclear power plants and nuclear weapons.

With this background in mind, we come to June and July. At that time, transiting Pluto at 8 degrees Sagittarius is opposed to (180 degrees apart from) the U.S. conceptional Uranus at 8 degrees Gemini—right on the Antares-Aldebaran axis and the nuclear hot spot. Under a Sagittarius influence, people can express resentment or carry out acts of revenge, often for political or philosophical reasons. Transiting Pluto in Sagittarius can stir up old animosities.

In addition, Pluto rules plutonium (the radioactive material used in advanced nuclear weapons). Thus, while Pluto is in Sagittarius (the sign of long-distance travel), there is a heightened danger of "plutonium traveling" as an act of war or revenge. There is also a potential for mass destruction—that is, destruction (Pluto) over long distances (Sagittarius). Add to this the Antares-Aldebaran hot spot and we get an increased possibility of war, nuclear war, terrorism and religious and ethnic persecution.

Upheavals and Earth Changes

On July 4, 1999, transiting Saturn at 14 degrees Taurus forms an exact square to the Moon's node at 14 degrees Leo. Saturn made a hard aspect to the

Moon's node at the start of World War II, indicating a breakdown in relations between nations that could be remedied only by the use of power.

On July 4, transiting Saturn also makes a nearly exact square to transiting Uranus at 16 degrees Aquarius. This configuration formed by Saturn, Uranus and the Moon's node is highly disruptive. It can trigger earth changes and cause economic upheaval, rioting, rebellion and the fall of governments.

On July 17, these influences are even stronger when the Saturn-Uranus square is exact at 15 degrees Taurus-Aquarius. Squares of Saturn to Uranus have historically coincided with major outbreaks of war. While this square influences all nations on earth, it hits the following nations especially hard: Russia, Israel, North and South Korea, China, Pakistan, India and the United States.

From August 7 to 11, transiting Mars at 14 to 16 degrees Scorpio squares Uranus and opposes Saturn. This transit could unleash or intensify widespread conflict.

Breakdowns or Breakthroughs

On August 11 there is an eclipse of the Sun at 18 degrees Leo. This forms a grand square involving the Sun and Moon at 18 degrees Leo, Mars at 16 degrees Scorpio, Saturn at 16 degrees Taurus and

Uranus at 14 degrees Aquarius.

In a grand-square configuration, the planets literally make a square in the heavens. This particular configuration is one of the most powerful of the twentieth century. It is explosive and could cause major earthquakes. It could trigger catastrophic fires and explosions as well as conflict and power struggles. This grand square is like the eclipse that triggered the Persian Gulf War, only much more powerful.

As a result of this eclipse, we could see an abrupt change in relations and relationships. This includes personal and professional relationships and relationships between organizations and nations. Not all people, organizations and nations will be equally affected, the variables being how this eclipse impacts their natal astrological charts, the quotient of good and bad karma each has, and how much violet flame can be called forth to mitigate the negatives.

This eclipse could trigger a painful *breakdown* of relations and could shake things up, so to speak. On the flip side, the realignment could be a *breakthrough* towards an order that adjusts to and facilitates social, technological and political progress. As a result, we could see a catharsis and a reconfiguration of power and social systems. While the astrology shows the potential for unleashing or intensifying conflict, it also shows the potential to resolve difficult conflict if there is a will to do so— a "breakthrough."

The eclipse of the Sun in Leo also signifies the passing away of bad leadership and the establishing of a matrix of a new, warmer, more Aquarian form of leadership. It indicates that there could be a new effort to take better care of our children and to raise education to a higher level. We will be able to find new ways of expressing ourselves from the heart. For example, there could be an increased recognition of the heart as the seat of wisdom and an increased appreciation of the heart as the center of consciousness.

Reactivating the Hot Spot

On September 14, transiting Mars conjoins transiting Pluto at 7 degrees Sagittarius. Pluto is still in a danger zone vis-à-vis the Antares-Aldebaran axis and the hot spot for nuclear energy.

What exactly will happen when transiting Mars conjoins transiting Pluto depends on what our karmic load is at that point. What is triggered depends on what forces remain unresolved. At the very least, it shows that there will be some kind of turning point, even if it's not obvious at the moment exactly what it is.

On October 25, 1999, Pluto makes an exact opposition to the U.S. conceptional Uranus at 8 degrees Gemini. Once again, this could trigger energies that could manifest as war, nuclear war, terrorism and religious and ethnic persecution.

Then between December 10 and 14, Mars transiting in Aquarius activates the square between transiting Saturn at 11 degrees Taurus and transiting Uranus at 13 degrees Aquarius—reactivating the potential energies for war, revolution and earth changes.

With God All Things Are Possible

Although these astrological configurations are formidable, I see a light at the end of the tunnel—and a way to make it through the tunnel more quickly. Again, what happens as a result of any astrological event depends on a number of important factors, including how much positive spiritual energy we can call forth to transmute the negative portents of these transits and configurations.

Saint Germain teaches us advanced techniques of prayer and meditation that can help us do just that. These techniques use an accelerated spiritual energy known as the violet flame. The more violet flame we can call forth to mitigate the negative karmic forces behind these configurations, the less destructive they will be—and the more their positive potentials can manifest. We will discuss these techniques in Part II of this book.

When faced with the challenging possibilities that can be deciphered through astrological configurations, there are two things we must remember. First, one with God is a majority. Second, with God all things are possible.

If we look back to the story of Sodom and Gomorrah, we can learn many lessons. Sodom was a city so caught up in fleshly pursuits that its inhabitants even tried to seduce two angels who were sent to warn Lot to flee the impending destruction of the city.

When Abraham learned that God intended to destroy the corrupt city, he bargained with God to spare Sodom and its inhabitants. God agreed to save the city if Abraham could find fifty righteous men among its population. Abraham continued bargaining until God finally agreed to spare the city if Abraham could find just ten righteous men.

This ancient account shows us the mercy, love and kindness of God. It does not please God to allow the full impact of our karma to descend upon us. But because he sees that we are jeopardizing our own souls and because he respects our free will, God allows our karma to descend so that we can quickly learn our lessons and progress spiritually.

Unfortunately, even though Abraham was

successful in his negotiation with God, he could not find even ten righteous men. Consequently, the cities of Sodom and Gomorrah were destroyed when God rained "brimstone and fire" out of heaven upon them.

What we learn from this drama is that each one of us, like Abraham, can make a supreme difference when it comes to saving our world. If God was prepared to save the wicked city of Sodom for ten righteous men when Abraham asked him to, just think what we can do through our good works and prayers when we ask God to work miracles with the violet flame.

5 The Handwriting in the Skies

Civilization is a movement—not a
condition, a voyage—not a harbour.
—ARNOLD TOYNBEE

Alfred North Whitehead once said that a civilization preserves its vigor when it is able to "adventure beyond the safeties of the past." He said, "Without adventure, civilization is in full decay."

Without adventure, without movement, we all come to a standstill. This chapter takes a look at the broad astrological cycles that will push us beyond our current limits into new territory. Like the wind on the sea, they can unexpectedly take us in a new direction. We can't necessarily hide from the elements, but we can learn to use the wind to our advantage and ride the waves instead of being inundated by them.

The Past Is Prologue

What happens in any given cycle is influenced by what has already taken place. "What's past is prologue," as Shakespeare said. In this case, there are three major groups of influences that set the stage for the first decades of the new millennium.

The first of these influences is the backdrop of our karma. We are at the end of a 25,800-year cycle and we are facing a karmic summing up. That means each of us must deal with unresolved issues from the karma we made during the last 25,800 years as we incarnated over and over again. I cover this cycle in more detail in chapter 8, "Passing through the Eye of the Needle."

The second major group of influences is the powerful alignment of four planets in the astrological sign of Capricorn. The third is the transit of Pluto in Sagittarius and Uranus in Aquarius. Let's start with the Capricorn conjunction.

Four Planets in Capricorn

On February 22 to 23, 1988, a rare and powerful astrological configuration formed in the heavens—the conjunction of the planets Mars, Saturn, Uranus and Neptune. This means that these planets were aligned at about the same degree of the zodiac. That conjunction is still affecting us today and will have a powerful influence in the foreseeable future. It initiated a period of potential upheaval and change on the planet with the promise of crystallizing a new social order at some time in the future.

Due to the influence of Capricorn and its ruling planet, Saturn, this configuration also indicated the start of an extended period of karmic reckoning. Capricorn tends to limit or bring to an end unrealistic behavior. The four planets in Capricorn affect all of us differently, but they signal that the testing of each of us personally as well as the testing of our planet is at hand.

Saturn, Uranus and Neptune formed the core of that conjunction, and Mars served to trigger the energies of these three planets. Since Saturn-Uranus-Neptune conjunctions are rare, they inaugurate long-term cycles and their effects may not be felt immediately. They also mark major turning points in history.

A conjunction of these three planets has occurred only twice in the last twenty-two hundred years. We have a clear idea of what happened during one of those conjunctions, which took place in the year 1307. If we analyze the events that took place during the fourteenth century under the influence of that conjunction, we can approximate how the present conjunction could affect us.

The 1307 conjunction initiated a century that is known for its violence and social chaos. It was characterized by bad leadership, anarchy, high taxes, the breakdown of social institutions, immorality and religious ferment and persecution. Corruption in the Church reached new levels.

The year the configuration took place, 1307, marked the start of a four-century period of global cooling called the Little Ice Age. The change in weather quickly disrupted the patterns of agriculture, and famine devastated Europe. Today, we too are experiencing bizarre weather with record-setting hurricanes, tornadoes, floods and droughts.

A Time of Conflict and of Transformation

The fourteenth century was also a time of conflict. The Hundred Years' War broke out between England and France, and the Ottoman Empire expanded into Europe. The worst disaster, however, was the onset of the bubonic plague. Known at the time as the Black Death, it was the most lethal disaster in recorded history. From 1348 to 1350 it killed one third of the population living between India and Iceland.

It is not hard to see parallels with today: inept leadership and heavy taxation, economic uncertainties, a rash of natural disasters, and religious persecution, otherwise known as ethnic cleansing. We also have our own plagues—like cancer and AIDS—and a growing struggle with infectious diseases as bacteria become ever more resistant to antibiotics.

Yet the fourteenth century also saw great transformations, and some of the changes ultimately led to the Renaissance. The Saturn-Uranus-Neptune conjunction caused a revolution in military technology that brought the feudal period to a close and hastened the rise of monarchies. Because of its enormous death toll, the Black Death started an economic revolution by consolidating wealth in fewer hands.

Pluto Brings a Sea of Troubles

Now for the third set of major influences that form the astrological backdrop for our future. We've talked a little about the transits of Pluto in Sagittarius and Uranus in Aquarius in chapter 1.

During Pluto's twelve-year cycle in Sagittarius (1996 to 2008), we can expect momentous changes in government, education, culture, religion, values and beliefs. We can see a dramatic transformation in the vision we hold of ourselves, our world, our place in the universe and our relationship with God. This transit of Pluto in Sagittarius also shows the potential for the repression of religions and new ideas, the possible outbreak of religious wars and cultures in conflict.

Another aspect of the influence of Pluto in Sagittarius is its impact on the astrological chart of the United States. Transiting Pluto in Sagittarius conjoined the progressed U.S. Sun[1] in Sagittarius shows a difficult challenge to the nation's president as well as to the office of the president.

Bill Clinton certainly has had his sea of troubles. In July 1996, when I first analyzed the astrological chart for the coming presidential inauguration, the nation was wondering whether Bill Clinton would be reelected or whether Bob Dole would win the election that November. In either case, I pointed out that the next president would face challenging astrological portents.

Ominous Signs Beneath the Surface

On the surface, the astrological chart for the January 20, 1997 inauguration had the look of a happy occasion. Jupiter (the planet of optimism) and Uranus (the planet of electrifying excitement) made a conjunction to the Sun in Aquarius. It was a day that for some was full of hope for future glory. Mars made a trine to those planets, showing confidence and strength.

There were also ominous signs in the inauguration chart. Saturn (the great tester and teacher) was in Aries (one of the signs of leadership). Saturn made an opposition to Mars, showing anger, loss and frustrated ambitions as well as probable aggression.

Of even greater importance, Saturn and Mars both fell on the axis of the Moon's node, which suggested loss and sorrow. The configuration was amplified by the squares (90-degree angles) that Mars and Saturn both made to the Moon. The Moon, in turn, made an aspect to Neptune, showing deceit, confusion and undermining influences.

The symbolism of this configuration could be interpreted as the "lack of a father." In a national chart, the father is the leader. These aspects suggested that the cause of the "sorrow" would likely come from the president himself and that the president might not complete his term of office, whether by death or dishonor or some other factor.

At the very least, this configuration pointed to a lack of leadership as well as sorrow and depression. Whether or not we would lose our president, this configuration suggested depressing energies that would hang as a shroud over the nation.

In 1996, I had no way of knowing how accurate these telltale signs would be and that by 1999 the president would have been impeached and tried in the Senate. Although Clinton was acquitted, he suffered a "loss" of honor, and the yearlong ordeal was divisive. It remains to be seen if Clinton will be paralyzed legislatively as a result of the crisis.

There are other malefic aspects in the inauguration chart. Pluto in Sagittarius fell in the seventh house of foreign affairs and war. At the moment of the inauguration, Pluto was close to its exact opposition to the U.S. conceptional Uranus[2] in Gemini.

This indicated that during Clinton's second term in office, through the year 2000, terrorism, battles, conflicts and power struggles might be on the horizon, waiting to be triggered by a transit of Mars or some other event. So far, we have already seen terrorist bombings of U.S. embassies in Nairobi and Dar es Salaam as well as confrontations with Saddam Hussein.

Freedom or War and Revolution?

Astrological configurations are interactive. Pluto's transit through Sagittarius will look different as it interacts with other configurations and transits—like Uranus transiting in Aquarius.

The influence of Uranus in Aquarius is hard to interpret. While it can bring freedom, spirituality, brotherhood and scientific advances, the last two times Uranus was in Aquarius were also periods of war and revolution. This configuration gives the impulse for freedom and individual self-expression, but improperly expressed it can manifest as anarchy, tyranny and revolution.

Take the case of Russia. In 1917, the Bolsheviks promised freedom, equality and brotherhood, and delivered tyranny. Today Russia is in an unstable, potentially pre-revolutionary situation, complicated by a shaky economy. But unlike the Russia of 1917, Russia is now armed with nuclear weapons. Other unstable and potentially explosive situations exist—in countries like India and Pakistan, for instance.

On the Edge

The most well-known nuclear close call was the Cuban Missile Crisis, but in May 1990 India and Pakistan came even closer to pushing the button. The Bush administration sent Bob Gates, a high-ranking intelligence official, to defuse the crisis. He succeeded, but the public didn't find out about the India-Pakistan crisis for three years. The Bush administration kept the information under wraps because it had allowed nuclear material to flow into Pakistan in the first place.

Experts say the situation could have become a catalytic war. It could have drawn China, the Soviet Union and the United States into the conflict.

Gates was quoted as saying: "Pakistan and India

seemed to be caught in a cycle that they couldn't break out of.... I was convinced that if a war started, it would be nuclear." Richard Kerr, former deputy CIA director, described the confrontation as "the most dangerous nuclear situation we have ever faced.... It was far more frightening than the Cuban missile crisis.... There was no question in my mind that we were right on the edge [of a nuclear war]."[3]

I didn't know about these tensions between India and Pakistan in 1990. But my spiritual teacher, El Morya, did. He warned that there would be heightened danger of a nuclear incident in April 1990. Prior to 1990, El Morya had directed my spiritual community to build fallout shelters as an insurance policy against whatever might transpire. We followed his direction and also held prayer vigils to pray for world peace and forestall any potential crisis.

I came under attack in the media for building those fallout shelters. And I could identify with what Winston Churchill once said about politicians—because the same goes for prophets. Churchill said an essential qualification for a politician is "the ability to foretell what will happen tomorrow, next month and next year—and to explain afterwards why it didn't happen."

When I read the news account of how close India and Pakistan had come to a nuclear confrontation, I realized how much goes on behind the scenes that we are not aware of. With probably eight nations now having nuclear capability, there is an increased chance of accidental nuclear launches or nuclear accidents, like Chernobyl.

A large percentage of Americans take out insurance policies in case of all kinds of eventualities—bad health, accident, fire, earthquake, flood. That's just what I consider a fallout shelter to be—an insurance policy. And so do many other nations, including Russia, Switzerland, Sweden, Norway, Denmark, Finland, China and seven Eastern European nations, who have varying levels of civil defense for their populations.

I have also been accused of predicting the end of the world. I don't believe nor have I ever said that the world is coming to an end anytime in the foreseeable future. The "end of the world" is just not part of my world view and never has been. I fully intend to be part of the new millennium. I look forward to the continuing spiritualization of our planet, and I have often cited the fact that Nostradamus predicted events beyond the year 3000, showing that humanity will still be around for quite some time.

The question isn't whether or not the world will

come to an end, but what will it look like in the twenty-first century and beyond—and what are we prepared to do to accentuate the positives and eliminate the negatives.

A Rare Megaconjunction

We're going to continue our journey through the heavens as we look at some major astrological cycles that involve Uranus, Neptune and Pluto through 2025. The reason these planets are important to study is that they have long-lasting, broad effects on most areas of life on earth. These planets are far away from the Sun and take a long time to move through each sign of the zodiac. Astrologers classify them as generational—that is, they influence entire generations.

These upcoming cycles will have a major impact on each of us and on our society as a whole. If we can calculate ahead of time which way their winds will be blowing, we can already begin to trim our sails to take full advantage of these winds when they arrive.

Our first stop is May 3, 2000. At that time a major astrological configuration takes place: the Sun and Moon as well as five planets—Mercury, Venus, Mars, Jupiter and Saturn—will all be in the sign of Taurus. The influence of Taurus tends to be conservative, practical and sensual and is often expressed as the organization of the material world as a platform for evolution. Taurus, for example, rules banking and farming.

Some of the planets that will be transiting through Taurus form squares (90-degree angles) to Neptune and Uranus in Aquarius, showing that the status quo will be challenged. Whether it's in our understanding of the physical universe, the way we organize society, our methods for managing resources or our expression of the arts, we will go through a dramatic transformation.

Squares can show an abrupt departure from the past. They are event-producing and sometimes violent. The old consensus, the old understanding of what is "solid," is going to shift radically. Just how it shifts depends on many factors, but we can anticipate a liberalization and spiritualization as well as a countermovement to suppress these new directions.

On a social level, the Uranus and Neptune squares will break the old social consensus. They can break the existing social contract and lead to the development of new social norms and a new "contract" between people and their governments. Perhaps it will be a contract at a higher level, but that is not at all guaranteed. What is guaranteed is that the old order is passing away.

We have an opportunity to make spirituality, information and technology available to everyone. If we fail to do this, we may face a serious challenge as the technological elite grow farther and farther away from a disenfranchised class of technological and information have-nots.

We are facing this challenge at a time when we are making a cultural shift from the industrial age into the information age—or what may evolve into the "wisdom" age. We don't know what it will look like yet, but in order to bring this age into existence we're being forced to develop a new political and social consensus driven by a new spiritual consensus.

As a result of the interaction of these forces, we could experience an "earthquake"—whether it's a social earthquake, a spiritual earthquake or a physical earthquake. Whatever takes place, it will be a dramatic transformation. We are changing the platform for our evolution for a long period of time in a significant way.

Although this Taurus megaconjunction exists in the heavens for only a short period of time, its influence and effects will play out and be felt over a very long period of time. It will be a turning point in astrological history.

Uranus in Pisces: Scientific Breakthroughs, Mysticism and Escapism

The planet Uranus transits through the sign of Pisces between 2003 and 2011. This transit combines the energies of the planet of sudden breakthroughs and scientific advances (Uranus) with the influences of the sign of mysticism, self-transcendence and self-sacrificing service (Pisces).

It can trigger a new way of looking at life due to revolutionary scientific breakthroughs and widespread mysticism or some combination of the two. For example, we might find that explorations of the atom, of DNA or of the cosmos might provide scientific insights that support the age-old speculations of mystics.

The signet of Pisces is compassion, giving, sensing the need of another and providing it in the most illumined way possible. If these positive influences become dominant, our society will consider it exciting to help other people. We'll see new communities, new institutions and new ways of becoming service-oriented.

On the downside, during this transit we could also see new, widespread forms or methods of escapism (perhaps a new, more pernicious drug epidemic) and philosophies that support individual license and freedoms (or false freedoms) that squander the gifts of the individual and enervate society.

Neptune in Pisces:
Self-Transcendence or Confusion

The next major astrological cycle we will consider is the transit of Neptune (the planet of mysticism) in the sign of Pisces (the sign of mysticism) from 2012 through early 2026.

The transit of Neptune in Pisces builds on what was accomplished during the transit of Uranus in Pisces. Thus, the impulse towards mysticism will intensify throughout society. People tend to view mysticism and idealism as impractical, but the real mystics have learned that the best expression of their mystical impulse is through reaching out to and helping others.

The keynote of this transit is self-transcendence, individually and collectively. If we don't properly harness the energies of this transit, we may find ourselves unable to take the next step up the ladder, largely due to laziness, escapism or confusion about what it is we are supposed to do.

The critical path to self-transcendence is self-actualization (to be who we really are) and service to others (to give who we really are). In this cycle, our collective initiation will be to serve others, to reach out and take some gift of the self and use it to help others so that they too can self-actualize and self-transcend.

Pluto in Capricorn:
The Redistribution of Power

Pluto moves into Capricorn in 2008 and stays there until 2024. During this transit there could be a dramatic restructuring and transformation of all forms of social organization, including nations and groups of nations, like the United Nations.

Profit and nonprofit organizations, corporations, churches, and other religious and philosophical organizations will have already gone through a dramatic transformation under Pluto in Sagittarius and Uranus and Neptune in Aquarius. Now with the influence of Pluto in Capricorn, they will be reconfigured. This will almost certainly extend to communities and perhaps even to families.

During this period of time there will be a redistribution of power and new ways to utilize power within all social organizations. This will give rise to intense power struggles. Residual forces that are holding onto the power of the old structure will come into conflict with those who are trying to develop the new structure.

Capricorn rules the old but it also is the bridge to the future. When Pluto goes into Capricorn, we will already be well into the new information/wisdom age, and the momentum of change will crush any remaining reactionary forces that want to drag people back into the past. Yet if we aren't careful, we could see the emergence of a form of high-tech tyranny. Pluto in Capricorn could also bring the development of social structures at a much higher level, depending on whether we've successfully made the transition to a higher way of life.

During a good part of Pluto's transit of Capricorn, Neptune will be in Pisces. As a result, the old order is going to be rapidly disintegrating (Neptune in Pisces) and another order is going to be rapidly crystallizing (Pluto in Capricorn).

The questions for this generation will be: Are these influences going to work together or are they going to work at cross purposes? Will there be two separate worlds—the Neptunian compassionate world and the Plutonian repressive world? Or will Pluto in Capricorn create structures that, like a beautiful platinum setting, ensconce the brilliant new diamond of Neptune in Pisces? We shall see.

While the first decades of the new millennium bring the potential for momentous shifts in consciousness that are both promising and progressive, we may still have to travel over some choppy water to get there. In the next chapter, we delve into a new area of prophecy with Nostradamus and Edgar Cayce as our guides.

6 Nostradamus & Cayce on Earth Changes

Nature has an etiquette all her own.
—LUDWIG VAN BEETHOVEN

The prophets who have peered into our era and beyond see radical changes in many areas of life—some that could even transform the very face of the earth. Nostradamus, for instance, seems to predict devastating earthquakes in at least two quatrains, which both refer to "the new city." He writes:

Garden of the world near the new city,
In the path of the hollow mountains:
It will be seized and plunged into the Tub,
Forced to drink waters poisoned by sulfur.[1]

X.49

Some commentators interpret *the path of the hollow mountains* as a street lined with skyscrapers, perhaps Manhattan. Not everyone sees earthquakes in this quatrain, however. John Hogue suggests that, in part, this quatrain alludes to the terrorist attack on the World Trade Center (whose two skyscrapers Nostradamus saw as *hollow mountains*).

The second quatrain that prophesies a quake is:

> Earth-shaking fire from the center of the earth
> Will cause trembling around the new city:
> Two great rocks will make war for a long time.
> Then Arethusa will redden a new river.[2]   I.87

This passage may even indicate a volcanic eruption. Hogue says that Nostradamus' reference to *Arethusa,* a Greek nymph who transformed herself into a spring, may describe lava flowing from a volcano.[3]

"The New City"

Commentators disagree about the identity of *the new city* in these quatrains. Some think it is New York City, which is near the garden of the world— New Jersey, the Garden State. Others say these quatrains predict an eruption of Vesuvius near Naples, which means "New City."

Los Angeles is also a candidate. As specified in

X.49, it is located near the *garden of the world,* the wonderfully productive San Joaquin Valley. Agriculture production in California is so great that the entire state could be thought of as the *garden of the world.*

Los Angeles is, of course, famous for sitting atop a number of geologically active faults, the best known being the San Andreas. Everyone in California knows that a catastrophic earthquake dubbed "the Big One" could occur at any time. How soon is anyone's guess.

The 1994 Northridge earthquake, twenty miles northwest of Los Angeles, was not "the Big One"— even though it killed 57, injured 18,480, closed seven freeway sites and left 25,000 homeless. That earthquake measured just 6.7 on the moment-magnitude scale. The San Andreas fault, 30 miles east of Los Angeles, could create a magnitude 8 quake, which would release eighty-five times more energy than the one at Northridge.

The California Seismic Safety Commission, the only state agency of its kind, says that there is a 90 percent probability of a large earthquake along the San Andreas fault in the next thirty years. According to the commission, we don't know how many major earthquakes could occur. There could be more than one.

"Two Great Rocks Will Make War"

What about the *two great rocks* in I.87? Peter Lemesurier interprets them not as forces of nature, but as two immovable powers in a battle whose casualties redden a river with blood.[4] Perhaps the blood of the victims themselves will form the *new river.*

John Hogue says these *rocks* may stand for the grinding of Earth's continental plates. Another commentator, Rene Noorbergen, says the *two great rocks* may refer to two lines of rock in New England. He writes:

> Geologists have known for many years that New York is, in fact, not built on very stable ground—although that ground is rocky. Commentator Hugh Allen [*Window in Providence*, 1943] made a disturbing observation, based on a study by William Hobbs described in "The Configuration of the Rock Floor of Greater New York," U.S. Geological Survey, Bulletin 270. . . .
>
> According to Allen, because of the distribution of the various faults underlying New York, Manhattan Island would, in the event of an earthquake, "break up into three large chunks, destroying all the major New York landmarks, as well as seriously affecting its millions of inhabitants."
>
> It is also disturbing to note that the faultlines

under New York City are part of a larger earth fracture which begins in the state of Maine and runs
beneath regions of Boston and Philadelphia.... By
the "two rocks" [Nostradamus] may have meant
the two lines of rock on either side of the New
England fracture zone, which will oppose or push
against one another in the upheaval.[5]

When I read these quatrains and this commen-
tary, I could not help but think of a similar prophecy
given through John the Revelator describing what
happens when the seventh angel pours out his vial:

And there were voices, and thunders, and light-
nings; and there was a great earthquake, such as
was not since men were upon the earth, so mighty
an earthquake, and so great.

And the great city was divided into three parts,
and the cities of the nations fell: and great Babylon
came in remembrance before God, to give unto her
the cup of the wine of the fierceness of his wrath.[6]

The Sleeping Prophet

Nostradamus isn't the only one who foresaw
earth changes for the new millennium. The changing face of the earth was also described by a celebrated prophet of the twentieth century—Edgar
Cayce, famed for the "readings" he gave while in a
trancelike sleep.

Cayce was born in 1877 in Kentucky, the son of a farmer. As a boy he prayed that he might be able to help others, especially children who were sick. He claimed to have visions of a woman of radiant light who assured him that his prayers were heard and that his wish would come true.

In those days, Edgar fared poorly in school. One night after his father had quizzed him for three hours on his spelling lessons to no avail, the angelic woman told the boy to sleep for a few minutes, promising to help him. He fell asleep on his schoolbook while his father went to the kitchen for a glass of water. When father and son took up the lesson again, to their surprise Edgar could spell every word in the book—and remember the page it appeared on. From that point on, Edgar memorized passages from all his schoolbooks in the same way, and none

Edgar Cayce
(1877–1945)

of the other students could keep up with him.

At the age of twenty-one, while he was working as a stationery company salesmen and insurance agent, he developed a gradual paralysis of his throat. The doctors could find no physical cause for his condition and could do nothing to help the young man, who risked losing his voice permanently.

Finally, someone helped Cayce go into the same sleep state he had entered as a boy to memorize his school books. In this trance, Cayce diagnosed his own condition, suggested the treatment, and was cured.

A Clairvoyant Gift

Doctors in Kentucky began to put Cayce's clairvoyant gift to good use. They found that he could successfully diagnose patients long-distance with only their name and address in hand. After the October 9, 1910 issue of *The New York Times* reported Cayce's miraculous powers in a two-page article with pictures, people from all over the United States wanted his help.

Over a forty-three-year period, the "sleeping prophet," as Cayce was later dubbed, gave fourteen thousand readings for eight thousand different people. He dispensed medical diagnoses and described natural remedies for many sicknesses. The people who sought his advice asked him not only about their illnesses; they wanted him to tap the wisdom of his Source about everything from marriage and dreams to careers and finances.

Cayce's remarkable readings, however, were not limited to advice about personal issues. Out of answers to seemingly mundane questions came profound teachings about spirituality and our relationship to God. Cayce himself was startled at the content of some of his readings.

A devout and orthodox Christian, Cayce revealed while in his sleep state—to his utter surprise—that reincarnation is indeed a reality and that our past interactions with others determine the course of our present life and of future events. His readings also contained unexpected prophecies of world import, such as how World War II would end, the future liberation of Soviet states, and the dramatic transformation of the surface of the earth.

A New Map of the Earth

One of the prophetic themes in Cayce's readings is the shifting of the earth's poles and the subsequent earth changes that could literally reshape the face of the earth. In one famous reading, he is shockingly stark. He says Japan will disappear into the sea and the upper part of Europe will be changed "in the twinkling of an eye." Upheavals in the Antarctic and Arctic will cause volcanoes. "The earth will be broken up in many places," and South America will be "shaken from the uppermost portion to the end." The shifting of the poles will cause cold and semi-tropical areas to become more tropical.[7]

According to other readings, many areas of both the east and the west coasts as well as the central portion of America "will be disturbed." There will be greater and lesser changes all over the country. Cayce said the greater changes would take place along the North Atlantic seaboard.

He specifically pointed to New York and Connecticut as well as Los Angeles and San Francisco. The main portion of New York City, he said, will disappear.[8] The southern coast of California as well as sections between Salt Lake and southern Nevada could be inundated by earthquakes, he added, but there will be more quakes in the Southern Hemisphere.[9]

New Breadbaskets for the World

Cayce also alluded to changes in land features in a reading that predicted which lands would become the future breadbaskets of the world. In this reading, Cayce was speaking to a man about his birthplace—Livingston, a town in southwestern Montana—and said the area "will have much to do with many, many nations." The prophet advised his client to become involved in the granary business in Montana and went on to say that portions of Saskatchewan, South Africa and the pampas in Argentina along with some parts of Nevada and Montana "must feed the world."[10]

Cayce himself had a dream that seemed to verify his radical visions. While returning by train to his home in Virginia Beach, he dreamed that he was reborn in A.D. 2100 in a town in Nebraska that was now on the western coast of the United States. As a child in his dream, he told others that he had been Edgar Cayce, who had lived two centuries earlier.

Men with long beards and thick glasses were summoned to observe the boy and they took him to the places where he had lived and worked as Cayce. They traveled in a fast-moving "long, cigar-shaped, metal flying ship." In the dream, Cayce noted, Alabama was partially covered by water, "New York had been destroyed either by war or an earthquake and was being rebuilt," and most homes were made of glass.[11]

Although Cayce's new map of the world seems foreboding, the sleeping prophet revealed that the earth changes that would take place during the transition between the Piscean and the Aquarian ages would be "a gradual, not a cataclysmic activity."[12]

Sunspots

Like other prophets, Cayce explained that prophecy is not set in stone. The changes we make in our own lives, he said, will have a great impact on what the world will look like in years to come. Some of Cayce's most insightful teaching on the human component of prophecy came in a reading about sunspots.

The periodic appearance of sunspots is one of the best known yet most mysterious of solar phenomena. An easily observed solar feature, they have been noted for centuries. Sunspots are actually magnetic disturbances on the sun's surface thought to be caused by magnetic effects in the sun's interior. They appear to be dark because they are several thousand degrees cooler than other parts of the sun's surface. They can last from a few hours to a few months.

The rise in the number of sunspots is accompanied by an increase in solar flares, explosions of hydrogen and helium above the sun's surface. Scientists know that solar flares can disrupt our telephone and radio communications, cause blackouts and power surges, and damage satellites.

Beyond that, many have associated increased solar activity with freak weather conditions, earthquakes, volcanic eruptions, flu epidemics, crime waves, riots, battles, arson attacks, political and mental instability and economic depressions. Periods of intense solar activity occur in well-documented cycles that last an average of eleven years. The sunspot cycle is now on the rise and scientists say it will likely peak in 2001.

A Blot on the Sun

Cayce saw sun spots, as well as earth changes, as a reflection of our own state of consciousness, a result of our own actions, the boomerang of divine law. His readings offer simple metaphors to describe that eternal truth.

When asked about how sunspots affect the inhabitants of the earth, he said that the question should be reversed. Sunspots, he claimed, are a reflection of the "turmoils and strifes" that we ourselves have created, and our own mind is "the builder." He asked us to think about what we have built:

> As what does thy soul appear? A spot, a blot upon the sun? Or as that which giveth light unto those who sit in darkness, to those who cry aloud for hope?[13]

Cayce said that the responsibility for earth changes lies squarely on our shoulders, and how we conduct our relationships with others has everything to do with the changing face of the earth:

> Tendencies in the hearts and souls of men are such that these [earth changes] may be brought about....
>
> As ye do it unto thy fellow man, ye do it unto thy God, to thyself.[14]

A bit like Hamlet, who lamented that "the time is out of joint," Cayce talked about earth changes as "readjustments"—adjustments that have to be made because something is out of alignment. Yet Cayce believed that just as we create chaotic conditions by our own out-of-alignment behavior, so we can create positive transformation by our loving attitudes and actions.

"In the final sequence of his life," writes author Jess Stearn in his book *Edgar Cayce on the Millennium,* "the great prophet saw the relationship of man to his Creator as more tangible and consequential than any El Niño or eruption of the earth."[15] Cayce said that we are not ruled by the world, our environment or even "planetary influences," but by our own free will. When we disregard divine law, we bring "chaos and destructive forces" into our life; when we are in harmony with the divine, we create "order out of chaos."[16]

Atlantis Come Again

Hundreds of Cayce's readings involve Atlantis, the lost continent that once existed in the Atlantic Ocean. The technologically advanced society on Atlantis, said Cayce, eventually split into two factions—those dedicated to satisfying their physical appetites and desires, and those who were peace-loving and spiritual.

The proud and sensuous Atlanteans began to misuse technology. They took advancements originally created to harness the sun's power for heating, lighting and healing and instead used them to control others. Cayce said their misuse of this technology actually brought about "volcanic upheavals" and the ultimate deluge that destroyed Atlantis.[17]

Cayce warned that mankind today, like the Atlanteans, are toying with forces beyond their control. "The early Cayce readings on Atlantis," says Jess Stearn, "revealed a highly technical culture that deteriorated because of the people's rampant greed and lust for power, turning them from the protection of the Creator they knew as the Law of the One. They became victims of their own self-indulgence. And Cayce saw the danger of man repeating the Atlantis disaster."[18]

An Age of Brotherhood

Cayce also made some interesting observations about the character of the Aquarian age and the choices we will face in the coming years. Like Saint Germain, Cayce sees brotherhood as an essential ingredient of this new age and urges us to walk our talk. He encouraged individuals, groups and organizations who have an ideal "to practice faithfully the application of this ideal in their experience and relationships."[19]

The most important thing we can do, said Cayce, is to "first know what is the ideal—spiritually." He warned that if people do not give of their means—their wealth, education and position—and do not live by the principle that "we are our brother's keeper," then a "leveling" will take place.[20] He told us we must prepare ourselves "for cooperative measures in all phases of human relations."[21] And those who will survive the stresses that may come, said the seer, are those who practice their spiritual ideals in their dealings with others.[22]

Finding Harmony Within

Though he couched it in many different ways, Cayce always returned to the Golden Rule as the standard. He emphasized, above all, our great responsibility to our fellowman. In May 1944, while the world was deep in the throes of World War II, someone asked Cayce what could be done to bring about a quick end to the war and a lasting peace. He answered, "The thing is to start with yourself. Unless you can bring about within yourself that which you would have in the nation or in any particular land, don't offer it to others."[23]

Sounding like a Taoist sage, he advised in another reading, "You must find harmony within self, you must find security within self.... Ye cannot create it about you until you have it within yourself."[24]

When asked what to do about coming events, Cayce invariably encouraged people to turn to their inner resources, the presence of God within. "Each soul," he said, "must turn within and seek its own relationship to the Creative Forces."[25] He also urged us to see challenges as opportunities for growth and soul development. Experiences that have shattered our hopes and brought disappointment, he said, can be turned into stepping-stones and become guides "into a haven that is quiet and peaceful."[26]

The Future Is Not Predestined

While some of Cayce's readings predict major changes, he saw his prognostications, like those of the Old Testament prophets, as warnings. He believed that the final outcome was in our hands. He saw several factors that can change the future—our free will, our harmony with divine law, our trust in God, our faith in "a divinity that is within."

When asked, for instance, what form the physical changes he had predicted for Alabama would take, he replied that it would depend in part upon the "metaphysical." He said that people's thoughts and actions often keep "many a city and many a land intact" as the people apply spiritual laws in their relationships.[27] And when asked what we could do to counteract serious events in the earth, Cayce replied: "Make known the trouble—where it lies, that they who have forgotten God must right about face!"[28]

Once again a prophet tells us that the future is not predestined. There is a window of opportunity before the mist becomes the crystal.

7 Is Mother Nature Mad?

> *People have got to understand that the commandment "Do unto others as you would that they should do unto you" applies to animals, plants and things, as well as to people!* —ALDOUS HUXLEY

Is *Mother Nature Mad?* That was the headline from a local newspaper one snowy day in December 1996 as 90 mph winds and heavy rain and snow pummeled the Northwest, causing roofs to buckle, power lines to go down and avalanches to block major highways. The headline—and the question—was more perceptive than many of us realize.

Since that day the elements have only become more capricious and more unpredictable. In the first eleven months of 1998, for example, storms, floods, droughts and fire displaced 300 million people and cost the world a record $89 billion—more than the entire decade of the eighties.[1] The American Red Cross spent more on disaster relief than ever before and the hurricane season was the deadliest in 200 years.

We saw Hurricane Mitch claim more than 10,000 lives in Central America, severe droughts and heat waves sear Texas, thirty-foot waves pound America's west coast, Yangtze River floods dislocate some 230 million people in China, and glistening layers of ice knock out power to 4 million people in one of Canada's worst national disasters ever.

A Wake-up Call

Why all the eccentric behavior? In July 1993, I received a call from *CNN & Company* asking me just that. The call came after months of calamitous weather that year too, including killer floods along the Mississippi, heat waves on the East Coast and record droughts in Australia. I was asked to be on the program, along with a meteorologist and a representative of Greenpeace, to lend a spiritual perspective to these events. Here's a segment of the broadcast:

CNN & Co.: We've basically asked all of you here to try to explain a series of very difficult to understand and almost unexplainable events. Elizabeth, what's your explanation?

Elizabeth Clare Prophet: Well, I think that we

are at the end of a 2,000-year period and also the end of a 25,800-year period. And in these 12 years, starting in 1990, we are reaping karma of the past 2,000 years and beyond and this is what we're seeing in the floods. I don't think God is here to punish us. I think that we need to learn to wake up and recognize that we need to take control of our lives and come alive and get into the mainstream of reality on our planet....

CNN & Co.: Do you think that we have brought this on ourselves in any way?

ECP: Well, I think you can look at life in terms of cause and effect.... There is a cause and effect sequence, and we are karmically responsible for our planet and the ecosystem. But we have to begin with the microcosm of self and we have to know that we are empowered by God through the divine spark within to take control of our environment and take control of our lives.

I think that there are so many injustices happening in the world that we need to be awakened by our karma. And when we don't listen to God and our prophets, then the karma descends so that we will pause and come together as a nation and face this disaster and find out what life is really all about in this decade....

CNN & Co.: Do you think this flood, as the

latest in a string of natural disasters, is going to wake anybody up and make them a little bit more responsible about the way we treat the world?

ECP: Absolutely. I think it is waking people up and it's awakening the flame of the heart and the love and the compassion, and people are pulling together....

You have starvation on the planet, you have drugs in our streets, you have violence on TV.... I think that that is why we have to be shaken awake, because we have to take more responsibility for what's happening to our children and to the people of the whole world.

I do not see these events as unrelated. They are related and we are responsible. And I do think it's a message that we need to find deep within our soul....

CNN & Co.: There are critics of yours [the three guests] who might say that you are using this latest natural disaster as a way to advance a political cause, whether it's better environmental care or a more conservative sociological climate. Elizabeth, how would you address that?

ECP: Well, I've been doing what I've been doing for thirty-two years and what I teach is the law of cause and effect that has been going on for tens of thousands of years on the earth. I think it's very important that we understand that there are problems greater than what we can deal with and that we have to have God in the midst of solving this problem. And when we see that it's a time of change and world transmutation, we can only call upon the sacred fire of the Holy Spirit to transmute the wrongs that we have done.

How can we clean up our sick and dying earth? How can we clean up the nuclear fallout and the dumping [of nuclear wastes] into the seas?

These are such critical situations that it makes us turn to God and it makes us resolve to be humble before the awesome influences that we've unleashed on this planet....

CNN & Co.: Do we have more weird weather, more natural disasters in store?

ECP: Yes, I think we do. We're seeing a period of intensification of returning karma to the earth through the year 2002. And I think it's designed to make us rise to a new level of being, to contact our Higher Self, to become one with that Higher Self.

One of the guests said that one day we're going to wake up and not be able to control the environment. Well, when could we ever control it? Atlantis sank, volcanoes have gone off. Man cannot control the environment or forestall a catastrophe like the one we're seeing in the Mississippi River or as we've seen down through the ages except through spiritual means. Earth changes are in store and we need to be ready for them by coming to grips with what is important to us in life. And what's important to us is the spiritual flame within. When we have that, we can solve any problem.

A Karmic Chain Reaction

There are two ways of looking at the roots of Mother Nature's frenzy. On the physical level, our abuse of the environment through deforestation, acid rain and all kinds of pollution has created a chain reaction that we never anticipated.

As Seth Dunn of Worldwatch Institute, an environmental research group, told Associated Press, "More and more, there's a human fingerprint in natural disasters." We are making those disasters more intense and more frequent, says Dunn. Hillsides are left bare after deforestation, and there are no trees to slow the rush of water and mud across the land or into rivers. "In a sense, we're turning up the faucets ... and throwing away the sponges, like the forests and the wetlands."[2]

A 1998 Worldwatch study said that the incredible destruction from Hurricane Mitch and the flooding of the Yangtze River were exacerbated because both areas had been subjected to deforestation. In recent decades, for example, logging and agriculture have robbed the Yangtze Basin of 85 percent of its forest cover.[3]

The risks we have so brazenly taken with our environment are big ones, and we have no idea where the chain reaction will really end. After the 1997–98 El Niño left its nasty trail of devastation, J. Madeleine Nash reported in *Time* magazine, "If El Niño's immediate impact on people has been hard to miss, there are equally important, if less obvious consequences for wildlife. In the oceans as well as on land, many animals are struggling to find enough to eat, while others—including disease-bearing rodents and insects—are unexpectedly flourishing."[4]

Our blatant physical abuse of the environment is only one side of the story, however—the visible side. Just as many physical ailments have roots in the mind, in the emotions and in karmic knots from the past, so do the ailments of nature. If we really want to understand the traumas playing out before us, we must look beyond the veil to the largely invisible burdens we have placed upon Mother Nature—beyond the outer symptoms to the inner cause of the pain.

Unseen Helpers

In the scheme of life, all created beings have a unique role to play. From the most distant stars to the smallest dewdrop, the universe is tended by invisible hands. Elohim, for instance, are the creators of life. Angels guide and guard us. And the nature spirits, known in esoteric tradition as "elementals," have the job of tending the forces of nature in the four elements.

The nature spirits have left their footprints in the lore and legend of many cultures, where they are described as everything from playful fairies and sprites to mischievous elves and leprechauns to grumpy gnomes. Most of us have never seen nature spirits—most of us who are grown up, that is. Many young children, because they have so recently come from the heaven-world and therefore can see invisible realms with their inner sight, have in fact adopted these little folk as their "imaginary" playmates.

Even Sir Arthur Conan Doyle, the brilliant creator of Sherlock Holmes, came to believe in the existence of these nature spirits, or elementals. It all started in 1920 when he received in the mail two extraordinary photographs of "fairies," supposedly taken by two young girls in the village of Cottingley, England. As Peter Tompkins reports in his book *The Secret Life of Nature,* Doyle at first thought these photos had to be a hoax, which Doyle, "donning his Holmesian fore-and-aft, determined to shatter."[5] After extensive research, however, he was convinced that the photos—and the fairies—were genuine.

"Doyle pointed out," says Tompkins, "that in the rational world of physics we see objects only within the very limited band of frequencies that make up our color spectrum, whereas infinite vibrations, unseen by most humans, exist on either side of them."[6]

Doyle wrote, "If we could conceive a race of beings constructed in material which threw out shorter or longer vibrations, they would be invisible unless we could tune ourselves up, or tune them down.... If high-tension electricity can be converted by a mechanical contrivance into a lower tension, keyed to other uses, then it is hard to see why something analogous might not occur with the vibrations of ether and the waves of light."[7]

As Tompkins points out, Thomas Edison and Nikola Tesla, contemporaries of Doyle, seemed to be on the same track. They both were trying to develop a device that could communicate with and photograph the spirits who peopled the fairy world.[8]

After much exploration and thought, Doyle came to the conclusion that mankind's cooperation with these nature spirits could greatly enhance the future of our civilization. "It is hard for the mind to grasp," he wrote, "what the ultimate results may be if we have actually proved the existence upon the surface of this planet of a population which may be as numerous as the human race, which pursues its own strange life in its own strange way, and which is only separated from ourselves by some difference of vibrations."[9]

Perhaps if Doyle had known about the elementals before he wrote his detective series, Sherlock Holmes would have enlisted the aid of these unseen helpers to solve his mysteries. And when the wide-eyed Dr. Watson would have asked him how he cracked his newest case, Holmes would have replied, "Elementals, dear Watson, *elementals!*"

Tending the Cycles of the Seasons

Those who have probed the world of the nature spirits tell us that the elementals are by nature joyous, carefree, innocent, loyal and trusting, and in past ages they served in harmony with mankind. But there came a time when mankind's negativity was introduced into their world, and their job became much harder. They now had to function in a denser world and restore balance where there was imbalance.

The weight of mankind's negative thoughts, words and deeds has been building up and building up over centuries and millennia. Yet the nature spirits keep on working heroically to purify the four elements—fire, air, water and earth. Day after day, they work to keep the earth on an even keel. Let's take a closer look at the four groups of nature spirits and what they actually do for us.

The nature spirits who serve at the physical level are called gnomes. Billions of gnomes tend the earth through the cycles of the four seasons and see to it that all living things are supplied with their daily needs. They also process the waste and by-products that are an inevitable part of our everyday existence. Mark Prophet once said, "I have become aware that every single manifestation in nature is presided over by elementals—that there are no flowers growing anywhere, not even a blade of grass, that does not have an elemental presiding over it."

Those who have the gift of inner vision and can "see" beyond the physical realm have described what the nature spirits look like. The gnomes, they say, are often short and impish, but not always. They can appear as three-inch-high elves playing in the grasses to three-foot-high dwarfs to the giant-sized gnomes you sense in Grieg's musical tribute "In the Hall of the Mountain King."

In addition to maintaining the cycles of growth in the earth, the hardworking gnomes purge the earth of poisons and pollutants that are dangerous to the physical bodies of man, animal and plant life—including toxic wastes, industrial effluvia, pesticides, acid rain, nuclear radiation and every abuse of the earth.

On spiritual levels, the gnomes have an even heavier chore. They must clean up the imprints of mankind's discord and negativity that remain at energetic levels in the earth. War, murder, rape, child abuse, the senseless killing and torture of animals, profit seeking at the expense of the environment as well as hatred, anger, discord, gossip—all these create an accumulation of negatively charged energy that becomes a weight on the earth body and on the nature spirits.

Like the tides of the sea and the currents of the air, all energy moves in rhythmic flow. Patterns of energy-flow between and among people, whether harmful or benign, must sooner or later recycle through the planet and in the process be assimilated and outplayed by the forces of nature.

Guarding the Gardens of the Seas

The elementals whose domain is the water element are known as undines. These beautiful, supple mermaid-like beings are subtle and swift in their movements and can change form rapidly.

The sea has many life-sustaining functions supported by the undines, who govern the wondrous gardens of the seas. The undines control the tides and have much to do with the climate as well as oxygenation and precipitation. Three-fourths of the surface of the earth is covered with water, so you can see how busy the undines are.

The undines also cleanse waters that have been poisoned by sewage, industrial waste, chemicals, pesticides and other substances. They work ceaselessly to heal the polluted seas as they recharge the electromagnetic field of the waters with currents of the Spirit. Their bodies are conductors of cosmic currents resounding through the chambers of submarine life.

The undines cleanse not only the physical waters, but also that aspect of mankind's life that relates to the water element—our emotional and subconscious world. They carry on their backs the weight of mankind's emotional pollution—feelings that are not at peace, such as anger, emotional abuse, unloving speech, selfishness, anxiety and indulgence.

Aerating Life with the Sacred Breath

The next group of nature spirits is the sylphs. The sylphs tend the air element, directing the flow of air currents and atmospheric conditions. They purify the atmosphere and aerate every cell of life with the sacred breath of Spirit. They are bearers of the life-sustaining prana that nourishes all living things. On subtle levels, the sylphs transmit the currents of the Spirit from heaven to earth.

The sylphs often have thin, ethereal bodies that transform gracefully into myriad shapes as they soar through the air. Sylphs are able to travel at great distances very quickly, and giant sylphs can actually span the skies and interpenetrate the earth, the water and the fire elements.

Like giant transformers, sylphs conduct the currents of the mind of God unto the mind of man. They also work to purify the air of pollutants— everything from car exhaust to toxic fumes emitted from factories and other industrial processes— before these can pollute the water and the earth.

The air element corresponds to the mental level of existence, and thus the sylphs also have the job of purifying the mental plane. The mental plane can become polluted by negative thoughts that feed hatred, anger, racial prejudice, religious bigotry, resentment, pride, ambition, greed, jealousy and other poisons of the spirit.

Infusing Matter with the Fires of Creation

The fourth group of elementals work with the fire element and are called salamanders. Their job is crucial, for they serve at the atomic level of all organic and inorganic life, infusing the molecules of matter with the spiritual fires of creation.

The fiery salamanders are tall, powerful, majestic beings. Their garments appear as pulsating rainbow fires emitting the full spectrum of the rainbow rays. The salamanders imbue the entire creation with the energies of the Spirit necessary to sustain life on earth. Capable of wielding both the most intense fires of the physical atom and the purifying, spiritual fires of Spirit, they control the spiritual-material oscillation of light within the nucleus of every atom.

Whether in electricity, firelight or the flame of a candle, the salamanders are agents for the transfer of the fires of the subtle world for mankind's daily use. Without the spark of life sustained by the salamanders, life and matter begin to decay, corrode and disintegrate.

The burdens upon the salamanders range from the weight of mankind's hatred to irresponsible uses of nuclear energy. Were it not for the fiery salamanders absorbing and transmuting the huge conglomerates of negativity over the large cities of the world, crime and darkness would be much more advanced than it is today.

The very sustaining of life—the air we breathe, the food we eat, the water we drink—is something most of us take for granted. Yet at the most basic level, we are utterly dependent on the selfless service of the nature spirits. The miracle of life is the miracle of the gnomes, sylphs, undines and salamanders.

Paradise Lost?

In past ages, angels, elementals and humanity worked in complete harmony. Mark Prophet once gave us a glimpse of that world when he described what the earth could look like if the elementals were not bowed down with mental, emotional and physical pollution. He said:

> If we had followed the divine plan, we would be able to see and be friends with the nature spirits. We would not have to deal with lesser or greater storms. The ground would shed forth dew to water our crops. No rain would fall, but a dew would appear from the air.
>
> The air would be saturated with moisture in just the right amounts everywhere on earth, and the deserts would bloom as the rose. There would be no excess moisture, and no lack of it; it would be just right for every climate. You would have the most beautiful weather and you would have the most beautiful flowers all over the world.
>
> You would have plenty of food and you would find that people would not be killing animals to live. There would be abundant fruit. Many of the fruits that would manifest are not even on the

planet now. . . . We would have communion with the elementals, and we would be receiving our instructions from angels.

When Mother Nature Shrugs

Today we have quite a different picture. Hour by hour and moment by moment, the elementals struggle valiantly to restore balance to an unbalanced world. When the weight becomes too heavy, they become burdened, tired, listless—just as we do when we are overworked.

When the earth, air, water and fire elements become supersaturated with pollution, when the burden upon the nature spirits becomes too heavy to bear, they are forced to literally convulse and shrug off the heavy weight. This can result in earthquakes, floods, tornadoes, hurricanes and, as a last resort, large-scale cataclysm. That's exactly what happened when Pompeii was buried under volcanic cinders and ash and when thousands of years ago floods ravaged the continent and civilization of Atlantis.

To draw a parallel, the same thing happens when someone you're in love with comes home and all of a sudden erupts like a volcano or explodes in a tirade, as if a cyclone just hit. It's unexpected, and yet it's been building for a long time. They've been carrying some burden, even if it's been invisible to you, and the longer they have carried it the more steam it has gathered.

It's not so much that Mother Nature is "mad," but that she is sad and weary. Like a mirror, she reflects back to us our own madness, our own craziness, because that is the only way she can get our attention. It is the only way she can shake us awake before it's too late.

The question is, how long will it be before it is too late?

No Man Is an Island

In a very real way, the outer turbulence we see in the elements is a reflection of what's taking place within mankind. The elementals have a certain plasticity to their nature, an almost chameleonlike quality that causes them to take on the vibrations of their surroundings. They mimic mankind and are easily influenced by our thoughts and feelings, both good and bad. Their mimicry of our discordant thoughts and feelings, generated both today and in the past, is what can cause raging floodwaters, biting winds, angry storms and searing heat.

A wise sage once predicted that there would be no wars on earth if we would resolve the warring within ourselves. The warring on the planet and the warring within our own members can go on for just so long without taking its toll. Jesus gave us the bottom line when he said, "With what judgment ye judge, ye shall be judged: and with what measure ye mete, it shall be measured to you again."[10]

No man, no woman is an island. Those who walk a spiritual path know that we are all interconnected. When we blow our tops or even engage against our better judgment in gossip or criticism, we add to the planetary momentum of anger, gossip and criticism that weighs down the elementals and our neighbors.

The comedy *Ghostbusters II* portrayed just how this can happen. At the beginning of the film, the "ghostbusters" discover a river of pink-orange slime flowing in an abandoned Manhattan subway tunnel. They determine that the slime is the materialization of negative human emotions—hate, violence and anger.

The slime begins to grow and multiply, gathering momentum as the population continues to generate negative energy. It starts pushing up through sidewalks, threatening to envelop the city and inaugurate a "season of evil." The threat can only be counteracted by positive energy—peace, love and good feelings.

The ghostbusters set out to galvanize the positive energy of New Yorkers. They charge the Statue of Liberty so it comes to life and wades into Manhattan. People come out in the streets and cheer, and the slime is finally overcome when the crowd sings "Auld Lang Syne."

It's billed as comedy, but it illustrates a truth: the negative energy we put out attracts more of its kind, and the longer we put off dealing with it, the more momentum it gathers. Sometime, somewhere, the snowball becomes the abominable snowman. Unless we seek and find resolution, that energy will, by the law of the circle, return to us. And once it becomes physical, there is little we can do about it.

Reverence for Life

What can we do to make peace with Mother Nature? How can we relieve the plight of the nature spirits? Given the high levels of pollution in many parts of the earth and the weight of world karma, it is a daunting task. But it is not impossible. We have the material and spiritual tools we need to do the job.

On a physical level, we as individuals and nations must, of course, move quickly to clean up existing pollution and prevent further pollution. We can all do our part, whether it's recycling or buying organic produce or demanding cleaner methods of burning fuel. The Aquarian age is an age of community, and it will take unprecedented cooperation and the mobilizing of inner and outer resources to bring the scales back into balance.

On a personal level, we can take responsibility to master our own negatives—habits that may harm ourselves and others and contribute to the mental, emotional and physical pollution of earth.

We can consciously give gratitude to the invisible workers behind the visible wonders of nature, whether it's in the blessing we offer before we eat our meals or the prayer we silently whisper before we lay our heads down at night. For without the unflagging work of the elementals, we would not have a physical platform to live on. We would not have a place to work out our karma or to grow spiritually.

We can remind ourselves and each other to honor and respect nature, the material world and our physical surroundings as chalices for Spirit. For, as Albert Schweitzer once said, "if a man loses his reverence for any part of life, he will soon lose his reverence for all of life."

Just as important is the spiritual work we do. Today we need an accelerated spiritual tool that can help us clean up pollution and transmute the karma that threatens to spill over into the physical. That tool is Saint Germain's antidote: the violet flame. In chapter 15, we include prayers you can give especially to alleviate the burden on the nature spirits.

Many prophets have spoken of coming earth changes as a result of the tremendous burdens on nature. In the following pages I have excerpted prophecies from the hierarchs of the nature spirits and Saint Germain. They speak of the nature spirits' heroic efforts to hold the balance for the earth, and they warn of what Mother Nature will be compelled to do if we continue on the same course.

More Than Nature Can Bear

In past ages when the discord, death and disease self-created by mankind have reached proportions greater than that which the elementals could bear, nature herself has convulsed....

The saturation of earth and the earth body with inharmony generated by selfishness manifesting in every plane and frequency has in the past and may ultimately in the present be the cause of the supersaturation of elemental life with more than even billions of their bodies can bear in a concerted and heroic effort.

Thus we come to explain that when mankind's discord reaches the level that is greater than elemental life can bear, the Lord God Almighty, acting through his emissaries...must release the divine edict for partial or complete planetary cataclysm.

(The Hierarchs of the Earth Element, April 6, 1980)

Turbulence in the Heart of the Earth

There is more than one form of cataclysm, as you have seen.... [Catastrophes have erupted] to show the people what is lurking at the threshold of consciousness and beneath the surface of the earth that must be transmuted, must be challenged, and must be faced....

Therefore elemental life, bringing to the surface then the turbulence in the heart of the earth, makes plain to all those who read the handwriting in the rock itself that this planetary body contains a residue of karma of molten lava and ash spewing forth....

Thus the beings of the elements react in the fury and fire from on high. And there comes out of the earth the message and the warning that is already come—that unless sufficient quantity of violet flame be invoked, elemental life will no longer bear the burden of the cross of planetary karma and there will be in this decade significant change in the very surface of the earth.

(Saint Germain, June 1, 1980)

Defend the Majestic Whales

Would to God that the murderers of the mighty whales might know the majesty of the mind of God and Mother flame anchored in these blessed elemental beings who command the seven seas and are the transmitters of cosmic light and cosmic rays unto all life abiding on planet earth....

Let the sacred-fire action of the violet flame restore the natural flow of spirit and spirit's fire to provide the alchemy of transmutation within the seas, without which there can be no return to balance....

Unless the sons of God rise up in defense of elemental life and the integrity of the earth body, certain cataclysm will not be averted.

(The Hierarchs of the Water Element, April 27, 1980)

Dangers of Nuclear Pollution

The misuses of nuclear energy and the dangers of nuclear weapons and nuclear power plants in the hands of those lacking the mastery of the elements under the four cosmic forces pose problems of great magnitude....

Mankind's current understanding of science does not allow him to accelerate the rebalancing and the reintegration of the disorders and discords intruded upon almost every form of matter by his reckless and wanton misuse of the natural resources of earth.

(The Hierarchs of the Air Element, April 20, 1980)

Sacred Places

Understand that the mountains of God in the earth—key mountains, holy mountains, shrines and focuses of the retreats of our brotherhood—are places where the pilgrims go, there to renew and reestablish the inner balance of the body..., there to enter into cosmic cycles. Thus the very air itself, the sun, and the fire in the heart of the mountain contributes to the purging.

(Saint Germain, June 1, 1980)

A Plea for Cooperation with the Nature Spirits

We send forth the warning to hearts of gold that unless there is a great intensification of the saturation of the earth body with the violet flame..., there will be in this decade major planetary upheavals, changes in weather conditions and earthquakes that result in great loss of life as well as permanent changes in the geographical surface of the earth.

The blessed beings of the elements have done and are doing all in their power to avert natural disaster. Again I repeat, we sound the warning! Unless the avant-garde of lightbearers will put their hand to the plow and join forces...on behalf of the servants of God and man in nature, there will be violent changes in the earth body.

We alert you, beloved ones, while there is yet adequate time and space for you to comply with the Law and provide the necessary counterbalance of God's consciousness and his sacred fire.

As electrodes in the earth, your dynamic

decrees, your prayers empowered by a pure heart enjoined to the Lord's Spirit, your fiats unto God's all-consuming sacred fire will be as the implanting of rods of the Lord in the earth, whirling vortices of energy that will consume and transmute mankind's discord by mercy's flame.

Thus it is our hope that by the conscious cooperation of elementals, masters and embodied mankind the course of oncoming world karma may once again be set back.

(The Hierarchs of the Earth Element, April 6, 1980)

The Great Tidal Wave of Light

Scientists and laymen, citizens and ecologists around the world read the writing in the rock of elemental life who have scored and underscored the faults and fissures of the earth with their mathematical formulae for the timetable of earth's changes. Alas, few among embodied mankind can read the hieroglyphs of *akasha*[11] and therefore benefit from the master scientists who move among elemental life as the guardians of planetary forcefields.

Nevertheless, the people of God on earth sense the coming changes. Psychics have predicted them more often than they have occurred while the co-workers with the fiery salamanders of our bands have invoked the sacred fire in the all-consuming violet flame to diligently remove the cause and core of those conditions which...could precipitate various forms of cataclysm—unless checked by the great tidal wave of light....

Let the children of the light cease to tremble and fear before the threat of impending cataclysm or even the law of planetary recompense. Let them rise in God to be masters of their fate, their astrology and their fiery destiny. Let them use the violet flame and strive for purity of heart....

The violet flame is the most effective and intense means of erasing the wrongs and hurts of the past.

(The Hierarchs of the Fire Element, April 13, 1980)

8 Passing through the Eye of the Needle

When the way comes to an end,
then change—having changed,
you pass through.   —I CHING

As I speak with people everywhere from all walks of life, I hear the same story: that it is getting harder and harder to cope. That they wish they could simplify their lives. That things are moving so fast they can barely stay afloat—and they're not even sure where the current is taking them.

Why does life seem to be coming at us with so many more challenges (opportunities) than ever before? For one, we are entering a new age. With the advent of Aquarius we enter a new era with a new spiritual vibration. Whether we consciously realize it or not, our souls sense that we have a supreme opportunity before us if we can just traverse the crosscurrents of our karma.

Spiritual Timetables

Spiritually speaking, Aquarius is meant to be a step-up to a new level of mastery. It is as if God is saying to us, "You have to master certain things before you can move up, before you can transcend yourselves as a civilization." Earth is a schoolroom and we are her students who have to take final exams before our souls can go on to the next grade. Before we can graduate, we have to prove that we have learned certain lessons and gained a certain mastery of our subject.

That means we have to review the lessons we have failed and retake our tests. Whether you call it karma or life lessons or a streak of bad luck, the challenges we are facing personally and collectively are a major rite of passage. They are meant to help us move beyond issues of the past and grow up spiritually.

In more precise karmic terms, our final exams require us to resolve unresolved issues of karma not just from the last 2,000 years but from the last 25,800 years. Why 25,800? It is one cycle around the zodiac. It takes approximately 2,150 years (one astrological age) to go through thirty degrees of the zodiac, or one astrological sign, and about 25,800 years for the earth to move through all twelve astrological signs.

So today we are completing our unfinished business not only from the Piscean age, but from the previous eleven ages as well. What's more, we have the awesome opportunity to pioneer not just the new age of Aquarius but an entirely new 25,800-year cycle. It is indeed a momentous turning point in our spiritual history.

A Preview of Our Life Review

The archetypal initiators of our souls who are providing our final karmic testing at the conclusion of this 25,800-year cycle are the Four Horsemen—impressive, awesome cosmic beings.

Like Paul Revere on his midnight ride, these horsemen come with a wake-up call. They are warning us that we cannot enter Aquarius as we were in Pisces. To fully integrate with the new cycle, we have to make peace with the past and shed outmoded ways that are slowing us down. We have to get rid of our extra baggage so we can pass through the eye of the needle. It is time, they say, to take responsibility for our past actions and to reap the rewards of our good works.

This accelerated return of karma is like having a preview of our "life review." As my dear friend

Dannion Brinkley (who had three near-death experiences and is still alive) tells it, at the end of our life we go through a life review. In that review we actually experience exactly how others felt in their encounters with us. If we caused them pain, we feel their pain. If we sent love their way and made their day, we feel that love. "You will become every person that you've ever encountered," says Dannion, "and you'll feel the direct results of the interaction between you and that person."

In a way that's what life is like right now. At faster and faster speeds, we are encountering the faces of our karma—in the people we bump into (and keep bumping into) until we find the key that opens the door to their heart or to our heart. Or in uncomfortable situations that demand our attention and will not take no for an answer.

Our karma, which influences the circumstances of our life, is the result of the causes we have set in motion in the past. The law of karma is impersonal. It brings back to us whatever we have sent out. If we have harmed someone in a past lifetime, for instance, we may meet up with them again so that this time we can help them rather than harm them. Or, in order to balance our negative karma, God lets us experience what it feels like to be hurt. He gives us a taste of our own medicine, so to speak—

a preview of our life review.

The reason it's important to clear our past karma is that karma slows us down. It clouds our vision and muddies the waters. It doesn't allow us to see clearly. When we don't see clearly, it's a lot harder to get where we want to go.

The Four Horsemen are the ones who are bringing this karma to our doorstep so that we can clear it up. When the Four Horsemen deliver personal and planetary karma, that karma unerringly seeks its target—the person or persons, one or ten million, who created it. The effect is going back to its cause, seeking resolution with its source.

At subconscious and unconscious levels, we have all heard the Four Horsemen galloping. Some shut out the sound of their hoofbeats and pretend that all is well. Others try to hide. But the wise welcome them, for they know that these emissaries hold the key to catharsis and spiritual growth. They know that the horsemen and the karma they bring are not to be feared, because resolution with the past is what will bring ultimate freedom.

A New Take on the Four Horsemen

What exactly do the Four Horsemen represent? John wrote down his mystical vision of the Four Horsemen in the Book of Revelation—a revelation that John says Jesus gave him, "sent and signified by his angel."[1] Revelation is a study in the psychology of the soul and a prophecy of the tests we all must master on our path leading to reunion with God. In Revelation's chapter 6, the "four beasts," heavenly beings, are sending forth four riders on four different colored horses.

In 1986, God revealed to me a new understanding of these horsemen and their role. The interpretation that I share is not the only way of looking at the Four Horsemen, for there are several layers of meaning to John's revelation. The vision God gave me has helped me better understand the law of cycles and the nature of karma. It has also helped me make sense of what is going on in the world and what we might expect in the future. Here's what I was shown.

As the vision unfolds, the thunder of hoofbeats precedes the horses and their riders. They are moving toward me in a straight line. Those nearest me signify imminent karma; those at a greater distance signify that which is yet to be.

The Four Horsemen are cloaked. I cannot see their faces. They are leaning over their steeds, man and beast one as they gallop through the night. The night is illumined by a full moon, whose magnetic pull on the emotions symbolizes mankind's vulnerability to their karma. Although the night is bright, the riders are dark silhouettes against an age of spiritual darkness. The age is illumined only by the borrowed light of materialism, sensual pleasure and a technology that the people are not the masters of.

A Pair of Balances in His Hand

As the vision unfolded I was shown that the Four Horsemen are the harbingers of personal and planetary karma. They bear that karma and are the literal embodiment of it.

The first horse I saw was the black one. He was twelve feet from me. An immense and awesome creature, his coat shone a black-silvery-green in the moonlight. Here is what John has to say about this horse and his rider:

> And when he had opened the third seal, I heard the third beast say, Come and see! And I beheld, and lo a black horse; and he that sat on him had a pair of balances in his hand.
>
> And I heard a voice in the midst of the four beasts say, A measure of wheat for a penny, and three measures of barley for a penny; and see thou hurt not the oil and the wine.[2]

The rider of the black horse is regarded as the one who delivers famine upon the earth. Why? John's description of "a voice in the midst of the four beasts" sounds like an auctioneer in the marketplace. He is auctioning off our wheat, our barley and our grain, the staff of life: "A measure of wheat for a penny, and three measures of barley for a penny..."

The "auctioneer" is quoting exorbitant prices that you would find during a famine—eight to sixteen times what the price should have been. The implied scarcity of commodities shows that the value of the people's labor (hence their self-worth) is being compromised.

The voice that John hears goes on to warn us to "hurt not the oil and the wine." To me this means that we need both the wine of the Spirit (Father) for our spiritual life and the oil of the earth (Mother) for our material existence to keep the gears of civilization running.

The black horseman, with "a pair of balances in his hand," is a symbol of divine justice. He is weighing the commodities of the nations as well as the karma of the souls involved in buying and selling. Thus the role of this horseman is to deliver the karma for the abuse of the economy—famine. Famine can come through economic problems as well as adverse weather conditions and improper food distribution.

From time to time in 1987, I was again allowed to see the black horseman. One September evening while I was conducting a prayer vigil for the healing of the economy, I looked up and saw the black horseman directly in front of me. I raised my right hand and called to Almighty God to stop the black horse. Then I saw the black horse rear up on its hind legs and stay frozen in that stance.

Just weeks later, awakened in the wee hours of the morning, I saw the black horse again. His forelegs touched the ground a number of times and reared up again. Five days later, in the middle of the night, I saw the black horse come down on all four hooves, race around me and go beyond me, the white horse galloping after.

There was no stopping either of them, and I knew in my heart that it signaled the descent of the karma of the economies of the nations. I was stunned and sobered, and wondered what would happen next.

I didn't have long to wait. It was October 19. Later that day the Dow Jones industrial average plummeted 508 points, a 23 percent drop—the largest percentage loss in market history.

The descent of karma starts a chain of events. Since that "Black Monday," the market has risen and fallen. We have seen reverberations from the Asian market crisis and the devaluation of the Brazilian currency. Some say the U.S. economy is still strong. Others do not. But whatever happens, in today's interconnected world we no longer stand alone. We are wed to other nations and peoples, for better or worse, for richer or poorer.

A Mirror Image

Each of the Four Horsemen is like a mirror, reflecting back to mankind their state of consciousness. The horsemen are like the guru who hung a mirror around his neck so that his disciples would learn that whatever they observed in their teacher was the mirror image of their own untransmuted self. The Four Horsemen are the embodiment of the collective untransmuted self of the race. Whatever they bring, whatever they do, is the reflection of what mankind themselves have brought and have done to each other.

The horsemen have personal as well as planetary significance. The karma that they bring corresponds to the karma mankind as a whole and we individually have created in each of the four levels of existence—fire (etheric), air (mental), water (astral) and earth (physical). These four levels are meant to be the vehicles we use to express our higher selves, but all too often they become polluted with our expression of the lower self.

If we look at the horsemen in this fourfold way, the black horse corresponds to karma made at the mental level—the level of the mind and the intellect, where the higher consciousness and the lower consciousness vie for the soul's allegiance. We can use our mind to bring forth enlightenment (and make good karma) or we can use it to manipulate and control (and create negative karma).

As the black horseman rides, he is returning to mankind the karma they have made by misusing the mind—through being critical, cunning, or following the dictates of a rigid human intellect rather than the impulses of a compassionate heart, for example. The karma of the misuse of the mind can slow us down. It can prevent us from accessing the most creative and intuitive powers of the mind. It can stunt the progress of our endeavors or hang as a cloud of black despair.

Whom Do We Crown?

In John's vision, the white horseman, with bow and crown, is a mighty conqueror:

> And I heard, as it were the noise of thunder, one of the four beasts saying, Come and see.
> And I saw, and behold a white horse: and he that sat on him had a bow; and a crown was given unto him: and he went forth conquering, and to conquer.[3]

Traditionally, the white horseman symbolizes victory. In the vision I was given, this rider represents on a planetary scale (among other eventualities) the United States engaged in wars small and great outside her borders.

On an individual level, the domain of the white horse is the etheric dimension of reality. This level of existence contains the blueprint for the soul and our mission in life. It also contains the record and memory of events.

The white horseman represents the perversion of our spirit. The spirit represents our calling—what we give our life to. Our spirit is expressed in our sacred labor, in the work of our hands, and in what we do that contributes to our community. Our spirit is intended to soar to the heights of the Spirit. The arrows of the white horseman attack our spirit and can demoralize us.

The color of the white horse is deceptive. White is traditionally the color of the "good guys," but the white of this horse only disguises his tremendous powers of deception. His warfare against the spirit is unseen and unfelt by a sleeping civilization.

The crown he wears is a false laurel. It shows that as a civilization we have crowned the basest desires and passions rather than noble desires and passions. Who is king to many in our society? Whoever has the most sex appeal and the most money. Who do many people worship? Those who can brazenly pursue their every desire, even at the expense of others.

The Power to Take Peace from the Earth

In Revelation, the red horseman is given "a great sword" and the power "to take peace from the earth."

> And when he had opened the second seal, I heard the second beast say, Come and see.
>
> And there went out another horse that was red: and power was given to him that sat thereon to take peace from the earth, and that they should kill one another: and there was given unto him a great sword.[4]

This description, along with the bloody color of the horse, shows us that this horsemen represents war, bloodshed, strife, and the amassing of armies and weapons. The domain of the red horse is the astral level of existence—the level of desire, the emotions and the subconscious.

The power of the red horse to take peace from the earth is the returning karma of mankind's misuse of the emotions through anger and war. The purpose of the astral, or emotional, level is to express the desire of God. Our feelings, or emotions, are meant to be positive energy-in-motion—intense feelings of love, kindness, compassion. Instead, emotions have been used to express anger, pride, jealousy, revenge.

The causes of war go back to the warring in our own subconscious and the divisions in our own psyche that we have not resolved. The apostle Paul spoke about the warring in our "members" that we have all experienced. He says, "The good that I would, I do not: but the evil which I would not, that I do."[5] The red horseman will have no power over mankind and no entree into our worlds if we will quell that warring in our hearts and souls and minds.

Slow, Sweet Death or Sudden Destruction

In John's Revelation, the pale horse is a harbinger of death, which is given power over a fourth of the earth.

> And when he had opened the fourth seal, I heard the voice of the fourth beast say, Come and see.
>
> And I looked, and behold a pale horse: and his name that sat on him was Death, and Hell followed with him. And power was given unto them over the fourth part of the earth, to kill with sword, and with hunger, and with death, and with the beasts of the earth.[6]

I see this as a prophecy of all things, actions and substances that lead either to slow, sweet death or to sudden destruction, including famine, plague, war,

AIDS, cancer, new viruses, suicide and the misuse of music or drugs, alcohol, nicotine and other harmful substances.

The pale horse delivers the karma we have created through the misuse of the physical level of existence. Our bodies and the earth itself are the gifts of God, the vehicles we have been given for our sojourn on earth. Without them, we could not fulfill our mission in life or balance our karma. The bodies of man and woman and the body of the earth are sacred, as Paul told us when he wrote, "Know ye not that ye are the temple of God, and that the Spirit of God dwelleth in you?"[7]

When we do not honor and respect our body or the body of others, when we harm or abuse the body, when we pollute the environment or do not care for animals, we are creating physical karma. When a nation engages in or condones such activities, then her people must deal with the return current of that karma.

A Karmic Racetrack

As we entered the decade of the nineties, I was again shown the Four Horsemen and another aspect of their ride. This time the horsemen are running on a large racetrack. This track is so large that when they are on the other side of it, they are galloping over the horizon. As the horses gallop around the racetrack, each one in its turn periodically passes the others so it can deliver a designated bundle of karma, for the Four Horsemen are on a cosmic timetable beyond our ken.

I also realized that the Four Horsemen have been delivering their 25,800-year package of personal and planetary karma over the course of the last 2,000 years. What was revealed to me is that the cumulative karma created by those who have lived on earth during this 25,800-year cycle actually fell due at the dawn of the Piscean age.

That karma would have descended in full at the beginning of the Piscean age had Jesus not stepped in to mitigate that karma in the tradition of the adepts of the East, such as Maitreya, Gautama Buddha and Sanat Kumara, who had borne this karma before him. Because Jesus chose to take embodiment and to fulfill his mission, this karma was allowed to descend in a series of cycles that would last throughout the Piscean age.

I had finally come to understand the full meaning of Jesus "bearing the sins of the world": Jesus perceived the pitiful plight of the people of earth and agreed to take embodiment at that crucial hour of earth's history to mitigate the full impact of the karma that was scheduled to descend.

His taking upon himself the karma that should have descended in full doesn't mean that we who made that karma are not responsible for it. It doesn't mean, as some Christians have misunderstood, that Jesus "wiped away" our sins (karma) or that he will "save" our soul without us having to lift a finger. It simply means that Jesus bought us time. He bore our karma for a time to give us the opportunity to gain self-mastery so that we could better deal with that karma when it descended.

Like other spiritually advanced souls, Jesus came as a mentor to demonstrate a path of self-mastery so that we could learn to become one with our Higher Self as he did. He helped us carry the load of our karma so that we could become strong enough to bear it ourselves. And that was our assignment for the age of Pisces—to become spiritually strong, wise and loving, to pay off our karmic debts to others, and to help others do the same.

Cycles of Time, Cycles of Karma

I also learned that as the Four Horsemen have been riding around their racetrack, dispensing our karma in increments, they have been moving through cycles of time. And the cycles are getting shorter, taking less time to complete.

The first cycle, which began 2,000 years ago,

took 1,305 years to complete. The last cycle, which encompasses the decade of the 1990s through the year 2002, will take just 12 years to complete (see facing page). So during their relentless ride of twenty centuries, the Four Horsemen have been drawing around us a tighter and tighter coil of energy that has been coming closer and closer to the physical plane.

In the year A.D. 2, the Four Horsemen began delivering mankind's karma created in the etheric plane. The higher etheric plane is the heaven-world of the planet, containing the perfect blueprint for life. The lower etheric plane is contaminated by karmic patterns and records of events on earth.

In 1307 the horsemen began delivering the karma mankind created in the mental plane, karma that has to do with misusing the mind and the thinking process. On April 23, 1969, they began delivering mankind's karma created in the astral plane by misusing the emotions, the desires and the subconscious. On April 23, 1990, the Four Horsemen began delivering the karma mankind have created in the physical plane through physical actions.

That's why 1990 was such a pivotal year and why the decade of the nineties has had a sense of urgency to it—because the final vestiges of our karma are being delivered. And this karma is much more physical than ever before. Here's why.

The Ride of the Four Horsemen

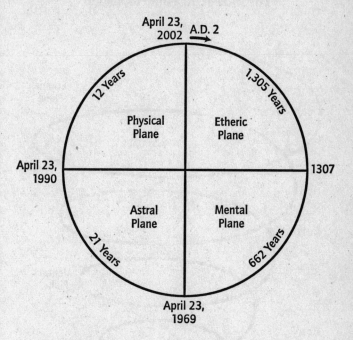

The Four Horsemen are delivering the negative karma mankind have made over the past 25,800 years in each of the four levels of existence—fire (etheric), air (mental), water (astral) and earth (physical). They began their ride in A.D. 2 and will end it in the year 2002. As they move through time they deliver the karma in cycles, and the cycles are getting shorter, taking less time to complete.

The Ride of the Four Horsemen

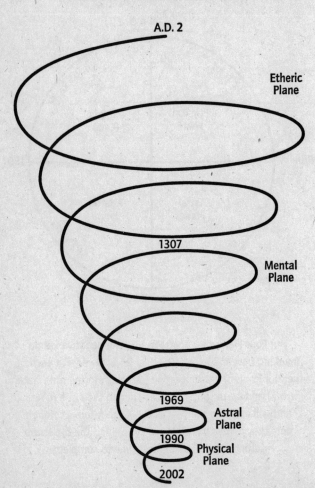

A.D. 2

Etheric
Plane

1307

Mental
Plane

1969

Astral
Plane

1990

Physical
Plane

2002

When you create karma in the etheric plane, 75 percent of it returns to you at the etheric level and 25 percent of it returns to you in the physical. When you create karma at the mental level, 50 percent of it returns to you at the mental level and 50 percent in the physical. When you create karma at the emotional level, you receive back 25 percent of it at the emotional level and 75 percent of it in the physical. And when you create karma in the physical, you receive back 100 percent of it in the physical. That's where we are today—mankind are receiving back, bit by bit, the physical karma they have created over this 25,800-year cycle.

The equations of karma are, of course, much more complex than this oversimplification, because the number of permutations and variables is almost infinite. Furthermore, many people create new karma every day, and they have to deal with that karma as well.

We Have the Spiritual Tools We Need

Now, before karma becomes physical it is much easier to turn back. For example, you can turn back diseases like cancer and AIDS when the karma that causes them to outplay in the physical body is yet lodged in etheric, mental and astral levels of your being. You can invoke spiritual light to consume the cause and core of that karma before it cycles into the physical.

One of the most effective ways to consume karma, and to resolve the cause and core of a condition before it manifests, is to activate the violet flame. Once a condition becomes physical, it becomes a matter of whether or not time will run out before the violet flame we invoke can complete the necessary cycles of transmutation.

The same thing goes for world karma. Nostradamus, Edgar Cayce, Mother Mary, Saint Germain and other seers have warned of war, earth changes and plagues for our time. But until a karmic avalanche actually descends, we still have time to turn it back. The pages of our future history have not yet been written. We are writing them day by day, moment by moment.

What is so amazing about the ride of the Four Horsemen is the incredible mercy that God has given us. Not only has our karma been meted out in increments over the last 2,000 years, but now that it is coming due we have the spiritual tools and spiritual awareness to successfully deal with it.

The Principle of the Magnet

We *can* transmute our personal negative karma so that it does not befall us as tragedy. We *can* navigate through the muddy waters of world karma as long as we are determined to resolve the internal struggles that beset us.

One of the best ways to explain this is the principle of the magnet. Imagine that you are wearing a magnet around your neck. Suddenly there are thrown into the room pieces of iron. These pieces are all sizes and shapes, from the finest filings to large chunks. Depending on the size of the magnet you are wearing, you will attract more or less of this debris. If you have no magnet, you may be in the trail of the barrage, but it will not cling to you.

Every one of us is wearing a magnet. The magnet is our negatives—our weak points, our bad habits, our negative karma, our buttons that are all too easily pushed. The debris of iron filings that is heading toward us is both personal karma and world karma.

Wherever you are in the world, there is a particular substance of karma that is being delivered by the Four Horsemen. If you have a magnet in yourself that is like that substance, you will attract that substance. Your magnet is also like the static electricity on your clothes that attracts dust or lint to you.

The lesson of the magnet is that when we transmute the karma we have made, we will not be vulnerable to the world karma because we simply do not have a magnet to attract it. I'd like every one of us to be able to say, "Through God in me, I have no point of vulnerability to the karma delivered by the Four Horsemen!"

Jesus told his disciples, "The prince of this world cometh and hath nothing in me,"[8] or as it is translated in the Jerusalem Bible, "The prince of this world is on his way. He has no power over me." Jesus knew we would have to be ready for the days when planetary karma would descend.

The principle of the magnet also works in reverse. By the same principle, we can also be magnetized back to our Divine Source. Our Higher Self and our good momentums are a magnet that pulls us up to the higher spiritual vibrations. The question is, which pull is greater? The magnet of our accumulated negative karma and our lesser desires or the magnet of our higher aspirations and higher desires?

Capitalize on Your Positives

I have looked the prophecies for our time squarely in the eye. Yet I still believe we can pass through the eye of the needle. Yes, dealing with our collective karma may at times be uncomfortable, even painful. But that karma is the birthing pains of the Aquarian age—an age full of brilliant hope and promise.

When people who hear about prophecies ask me, "Where do we go from here?" I tell them:

Commune with God daily, whatever your religion or spiritual path. With a tremendous intensity of love, make contact with the divine spark that dwells within your heart. Send that love out to the world. Pray for peace on earth and for the angels to bring hope to the world. Ask God daily to send the violet flame to transmute and neutralize our negative karma. Then go out and serve others with all of your heart—anywhere and everywhere that you can make a difference.

9

The Queen of Angels Reaches Out

[Mary's seers] say that . . . life in the world will change. Afterwards, men will believe like in ancient times. What will change and how it will change, we don't know.

—FATHER TOMISLAV VLASIC

In the twentieth century alone, more than two hundred appearances of Mary, the Mother of Jesus, have been reported in over thirty countries. Some claim Mary has appeared to them as they pray. Others say they have watched her statues "weep" or have seen her images on walls or windows. And some tell us that Mary has revealed to them urgent prophecies and secrets.

Mary has entrusted her messages to unlikely ambassadors—not prelates or popes, presidents or politicians, but children and simple folk. Innocent ones who could receive her messages in humility and convey them with undiluted simplicity.

This chapter focuses on two of Mary's apparitions (appearances) that have special meaning for our time. In both cases Mary chose to deliver her prophecies through children.

An Angel and a Beautiful Lady

In 1917, World War I was raging in Europe. In Russia, the Bolsheviks were plotting their October revolution, and Portugal was making a rocky transition through a series of unstable regimes. Against this backdrop of turmoil, Mary unveiled her plan for peace to three shepherd children outside a small village in Portugal. But first she sent them an angel.

Lucia dos Santos, ten, and her cousins Francisco Marto, nine, and Jacinta Marto, seven, lived in the little village of Aljustrel, near Fátima. Together they tended their families' combined flocks of sheep. One summer morning, as the sheep nibbled in a grassy field and the children played games nearby, the sky became dark and a strong wind came up. Suddenly they saw a light high above the trees moving toward them. When the radiance came closer they saw what looked like a young man, fourteen to fifteen years of age. He was "whiter than snow, transparent as crystal when the sun shines through it," Lucia wrote in her memoirs.[1]

When the children first saw him, they were speechless. "Don't be afraid," he said to them. "I am the Angel of Peace. Pray with me." The angel taught the children how to pray and then disappeared. He visited them two more times, asking them to pray a great deal and to continually offer sacrifices to God.

On May 13, 1917, as the children were tending their flocks, they had another extraordinary experience. This time they were startled by a brilliant flash. Thinking it was lightning, they ran for cover. A second flash sent them scurrying off in another direction. Suddenly they stopped. Before them, on top of a small tree, they saw a ball of light. Inside the ball was a beautiful lady.

As Lucia later wrote, "It was a lady dressed all in white, more brilliant than the sun, shedding rays of light clearer and stronger than a crystal glass filled with a most sparkling water and pierced by the burning rays of the sun."[2] In an interview decades later, Lucia said that on the lady's garments "there was no border of gold, no ornamentation" and that she seemed to be "made all of light."[3] Whereas the angel made the children feel "overpowered," Lucia said, "Our Lady always made us feel light and joyous."[4]

The beautiful lady told the children she had

come from heaven. She asked them to pray for the conversion of sinners and to accept the sufferings God would choose to give them. She also asked them to recite the rosary every day to "bring peace to the world and the end of the war." The radiant figure directed the children to return on the thirteenth day of the next five months and promised to reveal her identity in October.

Kidnapped

At first, the children's tales of Mary's appearances were met with disbelief. Lucia's own mother scolded her for spreading such a "hoax" and tried to get her to publicly recant. The parish priest thought the visitations might even be the work of the devil.

The ecclesiastical authorities in Portugal remained reserved and aloof. The Cardinal Patriarch of Lisbon even went so far as to forbid the clergy from taking part in any of the gatherings for the monthly appearances. Despite this reaction by the authorities, an ever-increasing number of pilgrims came to visit the site of the apparitions or to be present for them on the thirteenth of the month.

Journalists working for the revolutionary government of Portugal, which had persecuted the Church since coming to power in 1910, ridiculed

Mary appeared to three children near Fátima, Portugal, in 1917 to reveal her plan for world peace. The three seers, from left to right, are Jacinta, seven, Francisco, nine, and Lucia, ten.

the apparitions. They claimed the apparitions were an organized plot to incite the people against the government and they encouraged the civil authorities to intervene.

On August 13, the date set for Mary's fourth appearance, the local administrator did just that. He kidnapped the children, took them to his house, and interrogated them. When all three refused to divulge the secret message they had received from the lady, he locked them in the public jail and threatened to boil them in oil.

In a final attempt to learn the secret, the administrator had the children led separately to their supposed death and told each one that the child previously led away had been killed. Through it all, the children remained unshakable and refused to tell the secret. Two days later the administrator returned them to their homes.

Although the children did not expect to see Mary again until September 13, she was not to be stopped from keeping her appointment with her faithful trio. On August 19 she appeared to them in a field about a mile from Fátima where they were tending their sheep.

Convinced that the apparitions were genuine, thousands journeyed to Fátima to be present for the September appearance. On September 13, Mary again asked the children to recite the rosary daily to end the war. She also promised that during her final visit in October she would perform a miracle.

The Miracle of the Sun

When October 13 arrived, some 70,000 pilgrims gathered to witness the miracle. The day was unseasonably cold and rainy. Many had arrived early, spent the previous night out in the rain and were drenched to the skin.

Shortly after the promised hour of noon, the rain stopped and Mary appeared and spoke to the children. Lucia asked her, "Who are you and what do you want of me?" The gentle but mysterious lady replied: "I am the Lady of the Rosary. I want a chapel to be built here in my honor. Continue to say the rosary every day. People must amend their lives and ask pardon for their sins."

As she finished speaking, the clouds parted and the sun appeared. Then 70,000 people, along with those in nearby villages, watched the inexplicable take place before their eyes.

Beams of light in every color of the rainbow radiated out from the sun, sweeping over the sky, coloring the clouds, the rocks, the trees, even the upturned faces of the throng. Then the sun started to spin like a huge wheel of fire. Three times the whirling sphere stopped and then resumed its frenzied dance in the sky.

But the drama had only begun. Suddenly, as if dizzy from its wild spinning, the sun began to zigzag toward the earth. The onlookers cried out in terror, not sure if they were witnessing the end of the world. Many fell to their knees in the mud. Then, just as abruptly, the sun climbed back to its normal position in the sky and became too bright to look at. The people in the crowd, soaked to the bone from the rain, were completely dry.

Five years after the apparitions, the Bishop of Leiria-Fátima appointed a commission to study them. In 1930, after a seven-year investigation, he confirmed the appearances of Mary in a pastoral letter and said they were worthy of belief by the faithful.

A Secret in Three Parts

During her appearances, the Queen of Angels, as she is sometimes called, warned of a great chastisement that could come to the world and outlined her plan for world peace: daily recitation of the rosary, devotion to her Immaculate Heart and penance. On July 13, during her third appearance, she gave the children a secret message. At the time, Lucia, Jacinta and Francisco did not tell anyone the details of the secret. A decade later, in 1927, Lucia finally revealed part of the secret.

Lucia described the first part as a vision of hell. The children were terrified as a sea of fire opened up in front of them. "Even the earth itself seemed to vanish," said Lucia, "and we saw huge numbers of devils and lost souls in a vast and fiery ocean."[5]

The second part of the secret was Mary's explanation of the vision. She told the children:

> You have seen Hell, where the souls of poor sinners go. To save them, God wishes to establish in the world the devotion to my Immaculate Heart. If people do what I tell you, many souls will be saved and there will be peace.

Keep in mind as you read the remainder of this prophecy that at the time Mary gave this message to the children, in July 1917, Communism was not yet a major force on the world scene and it had not yet persecuted the religious. Mary went on to say:

> This war [World War I] is going to end, but if people do not cease offending God, not much time will elapse and during the Pontificate of Pius XI another and more terrible war will begin.
>
> When you shall see a night illumined by an unknown light, know that this is the great sign from God that the chastisement of the world for its many

transgressions is at hand through war, famine, persecution of the Church and of the Holy Father.

To prevent this, I shall come to ask for the consecration of Russia to my Immaculate Heart and the Communion of reparation on the First Saturdays [of the month].

If my requests are heard, Russia will be converted and there will be peace. If not, she will spread her errors throughout the entire world, provoking wars and persecution of the Church. The good will suffer martyrdom; the Holy Father will suffer much; different nations will be annihilated.

But in the end my Immaculate Heart will triumph. The Holy Father will consecrate Russia to me, and it will be converted and some time of peace will be granted to humanity.[6]

Just a little over three months later, the Bolsheviks seized power in Russia. In 1918 the Czar and his family were executed, and by 1922 the U.S.S.R. was established.

In 1929 Mary came to Lucia, now a nun, with her request: "The moment has come in which God asks the Holy Father, in union with all the Bishops of the world, to make the consecration of Russia to my Immaculate Heart, promising to save it by this means."[7] Lucia obediently wrote down the message and gave it to her confessor, who passed it on to the bishop. Some time later, the message was delivered to the pope, but it wasn't acted on for several years.

The "Unknown Light"

On the evening of January 25, 1938, the "unknown light" that Mary said would presage war, famine and persecution became a reality. That night an ominous red glow lit the entire sky for five hours. Lucia could see it from her convent window. The phenomenon was seen throughout Europe and part of America, Asia and Africa.

Scientists tried to explain the red glow as an extraordinary manifestation of the aurora borealis. "I think if they investigated the matter," commented Lucia, "they would discover that, in the form in which it appeared, it could not possibly have been an aurora borealis."[8]

Less than two months later, on March 12, 1938, Hitler invaded Austria. On September 1, 1939, he invaded Poland. Britain and France responded by declaring war.

Starting in 1942, various popes have made various blessings. Yet, amazingly, they have never done it exactly as Mary directed—with the pope and all the bishops consecrating Russia at the same time— even though Lucia has repeatedly urged this.

In 1994, for instance, Pope John Paul II consecrated the world to the Immaculate Heart. According to Lucia herself, however, this did not fulfill Mary's request because "there was no participation of all the bishops, and there was no mention of Russia."[9]

Many attribute the subsequent tearing down of the Berlin Wall and the dissolving of the Soviet Union to the 1994 consecration. Others, however, say the consecration has never been made as requested and therefore Russia is still a threat to world peace.

The highest-ranking Russian military intelligence officer ever to defect said recently that today Russia is "on the edge of social explosion." Her leaders, he adds, still act as if the Cold War never ended.[10] Even if that weren't the case, the fighting in Chechnya and the bloody war in the former Yugoslavia, leaving over 250,000 people dead and more than two million refugees, as well as the "ethnic cleansing" in Kosovo province are all painful reminders that there is still much instability following the breakup of the former Soviet Union.

The Controversial "Third Secret"

The third part of the "secret" that Mary gave the children during her July 13 visitation is popularly known as the Third Secret. It has never been publicly revealed. Lucia wrote down that secret in late 1943 or early 1944, and the message was sealed and stored in the archives of the Bishop of Leiria-Fátima and later sent on to Rome.

Lucia stated that the secret was to be opened in 1960 or after her death, whichever came first. Pope John XXIII read the secret, but 1960 came and went with no word from him or the Church about the secret. The message that Mary wanted revealed to the world remains shrouded in mystery to this day.

More than four million people have petitioned the pope to properly consecrate Russia as directed by Mary. Many others are pushing to have the Third Secret publicly disclosed. The Vatican's stony silence over the Third Secret has, of course, caused much speculation about its contents.

In 1963 the German newspaper *Neues Europa* published what it claimed was an extract from this message. Its version of the message foretells nuclear war, holocaust or at least major world changes. It also includes a severe warning that the Church and mankind must challenge entrenched evil wherever it appears. Whether or not this version is the authentic secret, these warnings are consistent with the tenor of Mary's messages given at Fátima and during her other appearances.

Frère Michel de la Sainte Trinité conducted an in-depth, four-year study of the Fátima prophecies.

He believes, like many other authorities, that the principal message of the secret involves a crisis of faith within the Church rather than prognostications of war or cataclysm.

Bishop Cosme do Amaral, the bishop of Leiria-Fátima, reportedly asked Lucia herself about publicized versions of the secret that claimed to be authentic. He said Lucia "confirmed to me that all this was an invention, and had nothing to do with the contents of the message."[11] The bishop also commented in 1984:

> The Secret of Fátima speaks neither of atomic bombs nor of nuclear warheads, nor of SS-20 missiles. Its content concerns only our faith. To identify the secret with catastrophic announcements or with a nuclear holocaust is to distort the meaning of the Message. The loss of faith of a continent is worse than the annihilation of a nation.[12]

The bishop may indeed be correct that Mary spoke to the children about the danger of a loss of faith, but what did she say would be the consequence? And if the secret were only about the loss of faith, why have the popes been so reticent to release it?

I must respectfully disagree with the secrecy of the popes who have read this message, especially when Mary asked for it to be revealed. Prophecy is given for the very reason that we *can* and *must* do something about it before it is too late. Mother Mary intended to galvanize the people and the nations of the world with her Fátima message, including her Fátima "secret."

According to Lucia, Jesus told her that he was unhappy that the popes had held back the secret. She writes: "In an intimate communication, Our Lord complained to me, saying: 'They did not wish to heed my request.... They will repent and do it, but it will be late. Russia will have already spread her errors throughout the world, provoking wars.'"[13]

Sister Lucia's own words on the Third Secret may give the best clues about its content. When asked about the Third Secret, she said: "It's in the Gospel and in the Apocalypse. Read them."[14]

In Jesus' Olivet Discourse,[15] he prophesies a "great tribulation" preceded by nation rising against nation, famines, pestilences and earthquakes— prophecies echoed by Nostradamus, Saint Germain, Edgar Cayce and Mother Mary. The Apocalypse (the Book of Revelation) contains many prophecies, among them the dispensing of divine justice (i.e., the return of mankind's karma) by the Four Horsemen through war, famine and plague as well as by the seven angels who "pour out the vials of the wrath of God upon the earth."[16]

Six Young Visionaries

Today one of the most controversial and celebrated appearances of the Queen of Angels is taking place in the small farming village of Medjugorje in Bosnia and Herzegovina, formerly a part of Yugoslavia. Mary began appearing to six youths in June 1981 and has continued her visitations every day since that time.

Why is Mother Mary appearing in Medjugorje? Perhaps it is because her requests at Fátima have not yet been fulfilled.

On that summer day in 1981, the teenagers saw what looked like an image of Mary atop Mount Podbrdo. She beckoned them and, as if pulled by invisible hands, they ran up the rocky hillside. As they drew near the image, they felt as though they had been thrown to their knees and began praying. The seers say Mary was incredibly beautiful and looked very young, about nineteen or twenty. Her light blue eyes were tender and kind.

After about ten or fifteen minutes, Mary left them saying, "Go in the peace of God." She returned again the following day, and by the third day huge crowds surrounded the children as they communed with Mary. Since then, some 20 million people have made a pilgrimage to the remote village.

Like the Fátima apparitions, these appearances

have been met with skepticism and persecution. The seers, aged ten to sixteen when Mary began appearing to them, were interrogated by authorities of the Communist government and the Catholic Church. At one point, the local police detained the youths, told them to recant and threatened to have them committed to a mental asylum. The parish pastor and other priests at first doubted the authenticity of the apparitions, leading one of the seers,

Since 1981 Mary has been appearing to six youths in the small farming village of Medjugorje in Bosnia and Herzegovina, formerly part of Yugoslavia. The youths say she comes every day and has given them messages and "secret" prophecies of what will happen in the near future.

Ivanka, to remark: "The only ones who do not believe us, are the priests and the police!"[17]

The youths were subjected to medical, psychological and psychiatric examinations to determine if their behavior was being caused by drugs, hypnosis or something else. Each time, the doctors found them to be normal and healthy. They were even examined while in a state of ecstasy during the apparitions. In a letter to the pope, Father Tomislav Vlasic said that when they are in the presence of the Blessed Mother, as Catholics often call her, "the youngsters do not react to light, they do not hear sounds, they do not react if someone touches them, they feel that they are beyond time and space."[18]

Playing Hide-and-Seek

Huge crowds continued to gather on a mountainside overlooking Medjugorje while the daily apparitions were taking place. The Communist government, alarmed at the religious revival, arrested several priests and nuns and for almost two years forbade anyone to visit the place of the apparitions. One day the police tried to stop the seers from going to the mountainside. The youths fled to the local church, and there in the rectory the Blessed Mother appeared to them.

The abrupt change in circumstances didn't stop Mary. She still appeared daily to the children in fields, woods, roads or the homes of the youths or others in the village. "It was almost as if Mary was playing the hide and seek game with the police," wrote one commentator.[19]

Since January 1982, Mary has appeared in the rectory, the sacristy and the choir loft of the parish church. If one of the seers could not be with the others at the usual time of the apparitions, Mary would appear to that one wherever he or she was. "We see the Blessed Virgin just as we see anyone else," say the youths. "We pray with her, we speak to her, and we can touch her."

Investigations and Denunciations

Bishop Zanic of Mostar, the diocese where Medjugorje is located, openly voiced his doubt about the apparitions. "The phenomenon at Medjugorje will be the greatest shame of the Church in the twentieth century," he said. "One can say that these are hallucinations, illusions, hypnosis or lies."[20]

In 1986, the commission he impaneled to investigate the apparitions reached a similar conclusion. Vatican officials, however, not satisfied with that investigation, instructed the Church hierarchy in Yugoslavia to undertake a second investigation to determine whether the visions were worthy of belief.

In 1991, the Catholic bishops of Yugoslavia finally released a statement on the appearances. "On the basis of investigations so far," they said, "it cannot be affirmed that one is dealing with supernatural apparitions and revelations."[21] In August 1996, the Vatican said that anyone could go on a private pilgrimage and could continue to organize pilgrimages to Medjugorje, but that these pilgrimages should not be regarded as official authentication of the apparitions.

However, Pope John Paul II is said to have a favorable view of the appearances at Medjugorje. In 1995, Vicka, one of the visionaries, went to Rome as the translator for 350 wounded and crippled Croatian soldiers who had obtained a private audience with the pope. He immediately recognized her and asked, "Are you not Vicka from Medjugorje?" He then prayed over her, blessed her and said: "Pray to the Madonna for me. I pray for you."[22] The pope is reported to have said several times that he would like to visit Medjugorje, although he has not yet done so.

Nevertheless, in 1998 Rome reaffirmed its former statement on the appearances. A letter from Archbishop Tarcisio Bertone, Secretary of the Congregation for the Doctrine of the Faith, was received in Medjugorje on June 24, 1998, the seventeenth anniversary of the apparitions. It repeated word for word the 1991 conclusion of the bishops of the former Yugoslavia.

More Secrets

The Medjugorje seers claim that Mary not only appears to them but gives them daily messages stressing peace, conversion, prayer, fasting, penance and a sacramental life. Mirjana, one of the seers, said, "Our Lady continues to invite us to prayer and fasting, saying: 'You have forgotten that with prayer and fasting you can ward off wars, suspend natural laws.'"[23]

This message hit close to home for these visionaries, who live in a nation that has been torn by strife. Miraculously, during the civil war that resulted in the breakup of Yugoslavia, Medjugorje remained unscathed. Believers say Mary was watching over them. Once a captured Serbian pilot said that when he flew over the village on a mission to bomb it, he couldn't locate any houses or the church. All he could see was what looked like a white sheet of light covering the village, so he turned back.[24]

In addition to her daily messages to the visionaries, Mary promised to give each of them ten "secrets"—prophecies of events that will occur in the near future. The seers say that when they each have received all ten secrets, Mary will cease appearing to them and that these will be her last formal appearances on earth. So far only one of the secrets has been revealed: Mary has promised to leave a visible sign on the mountain where she first appeared. "When the sign comes," said Mary, "it will be too late for many."

Life in the World Will Change

In an August 1983 interview Father Vlasic said that, based on the secrets entrusted to them, the seers say, "Life in the world will change. Afterwards, men will believe like in ancient times. What will change and how it will change, we don't know until the secrets are revealed."[25]

On November 30, 1983, the seer Marija told her spiritual director, Father Vlasic, that Mary wanted the pope and bishop "to be advised immediately of the urgency and importance of the message of Medjugorje." A few days later, Father Vlasic sent a report to the pope and the bishop of Mostar. In it he gave the following account from a conversation he had with another of the seers, Mirjana.

As you will see, the themes of this message echo Mary's Fátima prophecies. Most importantly, they tell us that we still can avert catastrophe through prayer. (Father Vlasic said these are not word-for-word quotations but the essence of Mirjana's words.)

Before the visible sign is given to humanity, there will be three warnings to the world. The warnings will be in the form of events on the earth. Mirjana will witness them. Three days before one of these warnings, she will advise a priest of her choice. Mirjana's testimony will be a confirmation of the apparitions and an incentive for the conversion of the world.

After the warnings, the visible sign will be given for all humanity at the place of the apparitions in Medjugorje. The sign will be given as the testimony of the apparitions and a call back to faith.

The ninth and tenth secrets are serious. They concern chastisement for the sins of the world. Punishment is inevitable, for we cannot expect the whole world to be converted. The punishment can be diminished by prayer and penance, but it cannot be eliminated.

Mirjana says that one of the evils that threatened the world, the one contained in the seventh secret, has been averted thanks to prayer and fasting. That is why the Blessed Virgin continues to encourage prayer and fasting: "You have forgotten that through prayer and fasting you can avert war and suspend the laws of nature."

After the first admonition, the others will follow in a rather short time. Thus, people will have some time for conversion.

That interval will be a period of grace and conversion. After the visible sign appears, those who are still alive will have little time for conversion. For that reason, the Blessed Virgin invites us to urgent conversion and reconciliation.

The invitation to prayer and penance is meant to avert evil and war, but most of all to save souls.[26]

According to Mirjana, continues Father Vlasic,

We are close to the events predicted by the Blessed Virgin.... Hurry, be converted. Open your hearts to God. This is a message to all mankind.[27]

The seers say that the secret messages contain both good and bad things and that they pertain to the youths personally, to the Church and to all humanity. Mirjana, Ivanka and, most recently, Jacov have received all ten secrets. The remaining three seers—Ivan, Marija and Vicka—have received nine secrets and are awaiting their tenth.

10 Mary's Plan for Peace

> We must seek, above all, a world of
> peace, . . . a world where peace is not
> a mere interlude between wars, but an
> incentive to the creative energies of
> humanity. —JOHN F. KENNEDY

Mary's prophecies and her plan
for peace are for everyone on earth—of every religion or no religion. For her heart is a universal heart
and her call is a universal call.

The prophecies she gave at Fátima and Medjugorje reveal the same message. The warning: the
world is fragile. Mankind's "sins" (karma) have put
the earth in a precarious place. The remedy: pray
and quickly make amends where you have harmed
others.

"World peace is at a critical stage," the Queen
of Angels tells the world through the visionaries at

Medjugorje. "I need your prayers.... I cannot help the world without you."[1]

Mary has also told her young seers to pray for the "conversion" of the world. She is not speaking about a "religious" conversion but a spiritual one, one that has its foundations in the heart and not in doctrine. *To convert* comes from the Latin root meaning "to turn around." Mary is calling us to "turn around" our heart, our soul, our mind to face the sun of our Higher Self so that the shadows will be behind us.

We can think of Mary as a sister who has walked the path before us, gained self-mastery and would help us do the same, no matter what our chosen path. She is also a prophetess and powerful intercessor who has offered to help us find the way out of our most difficult karmic dilemmas.

At Fátima, Mary outlined three specific steps to bring about world peace: recitation of the rosary, devotion to her Immaculate Heart, and penance. Remember, she was speaking to her little messengers at Fátima in terms they could understand. But again, all three solutions go far beyond the boundaries of Catholicism or any ism. They describe the essential ingredients of any spiritual path: cultivating an inner spiritual life (through meditation, heartfelt prayer and devotion) and living a practical spiritual life (by helping others).

A Miraculous Escape

In her many appearances throughout the world, Mary has stressed over and over again that the rosary is key to bringing about world peace. One of the most stunning examples of the miraculous power of the rosary is from World War II. When the atomic bomb was dropped on Hiroshima in 1945, about 80,000 people died instantly. Everyone within a mile radius perished from the searing blast—except eight men who were living near the center of the blinding nuclear flash. Others living farther away continued to die from the lethal effects of the radiation, but not these men.

Since then, some two hundred scientists have examined the eight men, trying in vain to determine what could have saved them from incineration. One of the survivors, Father H. Shiffner, S.J., gave the dramatic answer on American TV: "In that house the rosary was prayed every day. In that house we were living the message of Fátima."[2]

Getting beyond Prejudice

I was not raised as a Catholic and I never understood what the rosary really was or what it could do. And, like many, I had a prejudice against Mary that had been drilled into me since childhood. I had never challenged it and never reasoned it through for myself. Like anything that we are taught and we accept early in life, it was just there growing inside of me. It all came to a head unexpectedly one day while I was a student at Boston University.

I was finishing my degree in political science and preparing to work with Mark Prophet in Washington, D.C. But before I left Boston, I was to have one of the most important experiences of my spiritual path. It taught me more about myself than years of philosophy or logic or psychology under the best instructors.

Earlier, while I had been studying in Europe, I had made pilgrimages to the Catholic cathedrals. Yet I still believed, as I had been told, that Catholics worshiped idols, that Mother Mary was some sort of a goddess who allowed herself to be called the "Mother of God." I thought people worshiped her in place of God. I was taught that people made her equal with or even greater than Jesus Christ or Almighty God himself. I didn't understand why you needed to go through Mary to get to Jesus to get to God.

I found myself reacting with intense feelings to the images and icons of Mother Mary all over Boston. One in particular was a huge mural that covered the wall of the subway I took to BU every day, bearing the title "Queen of the Universe." If she

was so great, why did she allow this blasphemy?
I was angry with her. With all of the other problems
that made for division and confusion in Christen-
dom, why didn't she come down and straighten this
one out?

I guess I was disturbed because deep down inside of me I really wanted to know her as she was,
not as others had portrayed her to me. It was in this
state of unawareness, ignorance and programmed
hostility toward Mary that she found me.

A Magical Encounter

One sunny day I was happily walking along the
sidewalk in the middle of crowds and traffic on a
lunch hour, thanking God for all that he had given
me and looking forward to starting the next chapter
in my life. All of a sudden I looked up—and there
she was. I was face to face with the beautiful Mary,
a being of great light—a transcendent and lovely
young woman, full of truth and beauty and integrity.

A charge of light and indescribable joy passed
through my body, traveling like a loop of electricity
from my head to my feet and back again. I remember the exact place in the pavement where I was
stopped—transfixed, transformed. She had the face
of a young maiden. She was Michelangelo's *Pietà*,
alive and well and glorious. Her heart was on fire

with an energy that she transmitted at will.

She was suspended above and before me, as real as you are, as real as I am. She looked like someone you could talk to about anything. She seemed just like me but in another dimension. Except she really wasn't quite like me. She was resplendent with the light of God that she had adored and become. She had realized a greater portion of the Self than most of us even imagine can be realized.

There was enough of the divine part of her in me, and enough of the human part of me in her, that I felt that I too could realize more of my Higher Self—if she would show me the way. I wanted to be like her, and I knew that I could if I embraced her and her path.

A Soul Awakening

Mary is someone who has walked the earth, successfully overcome the trials and tribulations of her time, and graduated from earth's schoolroom. She is someone who can teach us how to be more of our real self, how to be one with God. She is someone who can show us that just as God has expressed the many aspects of his personality in what we have come to call Father, Son, Holy Spirit, Christ or Buddha, the divine can also dress itself in the garb of Mother.

Mother Mary is one among many heavenly

hosts—including Kuan Yin, Kali or Tara in the East —who have understood and come to exemplify the feminine principle of God. They have personified the nurturing, loving, comforting aspect of God that we call "Mother."

As I stood before Mary, she poured out to me the love of her heart. In the presence of her immense compassion I was being wrapped in the swaddling garment of her understanding. Mary was my friend. In my inner soul I had always loved her, but my outer mind had been programmed. How could such a dichotomy exist in one person?

I became so enamored with Mother Mary that I didn't walk but ran to the nearest Catholic church. I went down the aisle. I knelt before her statue in full awareness that I was kneeling before a representation of the Divine Mother. I was not worshiping the statue and I was not worshiping Mother Mary. I was bowing in gratitude for the light within her, the light of the One God that had manifest itself to me as the Mother whom Mary had become. I could feel her love flowing to me and her forgiveness dissolving all misunderstanding.

Nurturing the Feminine

Ever since that moment I have felt the presence of Mother Mary with me, teaching me that we must all learn to nurture the feminine aspect of our being. "This is the age of the awareness of God as Mother," Mary tells us. To "mother" as God would mother is to nourish all life on earth. When we realize our feminine potential, we too will be able to nourish life, first in ourselves and then in one another.

The Aquarian age is the age of the Mother and the Holy Spirit. It is the age when we are meant to experience and express the Mother aspect of God. Coming to understand this feminine aspect of God can liberate the creative feminine energy within us, man or woman—the energy of beauty and creativity, intuition and inspiration.

The concept of God as "Mother" is not new to Eastern spirituality. The Hindus meditate upon Mother as the Goddess Kundalini, describing her as the white light, or the coiled serpent, that rises from the base of the spine to the crown, activating levels of spiritual consciousness in each of the chakras (spiritual centers) through which that light passes along the way.

Whether we are male or female, we are intended to raise this sacred light of our innermost being that lies dormant within us. The key to unlocking this energy, the Kundalini, is adoration of the Mother Principle.

Mother Mary has assured me that the raising of the Kundalini is indeed a part of Western tradition, and this is why she appeared to several of the saints with the safe and sound method of raising the Mother light through the rosary. The saints have been portrayed with a white light, or halo, around their heads, because they have raised the Kundalini and opened their crown chakras. They have entered into the bliss of God.

We know that the great Christian mystics such as Saint John of the Cross, Saint Thérèse of Lisieux and Padre Pio have all had this inner experience— so filled with the divine passion, the bliss of the Beloved, as to defy comprehension.

A New Rosary

In the fall of 1972 as I was meditating, Mother Mary came to me and dictated what she called her "Scriptural Rosary for the New Age." This is a non-denominational ritual. Mary said she wanted it to be used as a universal adoration of the Mother principle of God by people of all faiths. Later she gave me a series of shorter, fifteen-minute versions of the rosary. These rosaries give us the opportunity to spend even fifteen minutes each day speaking to Mother Mary and turning over to her our personal burdens and the burdens of the world.

Mary, Queen of Angels and Queen of Peace

In Mary's new-age scriptural rosary, the Hail Mary prayer is different from the traditional Catholic version. She replaced the word "sinners" with "sons and daughters of God" and replaced the words "now and at the hour of our death" with "now and at the hour of our victory over sin, disease and death." She said it was important not to continually accept the label of "sinner" but to affirm our true identity as victorious sons and daughters of God.

So the Hail Mary in the new rosary reads: "Hail, Mary, full of grace, the Lord is with thee. Blessed art thou among women and blessed is the fruit of thy womb, Jesus. Holy Mary, Mother of God, pray for us, sons and daughters of God, now and at the hour of our victory over sin, disease and death."

Mary told me that when we say, "Hail, Mary!" it means "Hail, Mother Ray." With this prayer, we are not worshiping the person of Mary, but we are greeting the feminine principle of the Godhead, the "Mother Ray." The Hail Mary, she added, is the safe and gentle way for Western devotees to raise the energies of the Kundalini for the unfolding of their soul's full potential.

If enough people would give the rosary daily, Mother Mary said, it would "give strength to every heart" and "prevent a great deal of destruction of human life during the days that are ahead." When we give Mary's rosary, we are taking part in step one of her plan to help bring peace to the world. In the last section of this book we have included one of Mary's new rosaries.

A Spiritual Interchange through the Heart

The second step of the peace plan Mary unveiled at Fátima is devotion to her Immaculate Heart. Devotees of Mary say that this prescription for peace is what saved their countries. In a spectacular ceremony in Portugal, for example, all the bishops consecrated their nation to the Immaculate Heart of Mary. Many of her citizens believe that that is what spared them from the ravages of the neighboring Spanish Civil War.

In addition, the only Spanish city left unscathed by that bloody civil war, whose widespread destruction and killing were unparalleled in Spanish history, was Seville—the only diocese in Spain that had been officially consecrated to the Immaculate Heart.

What is the "Immaculate Heart of Mary"? Statues of the Blessed Mother show her heart either surrounded with roses (recalling her virtues), pierced by swords (representing the sorrows she experienced as the mother of Jesus) or surrounded with thorns (signifying her sorrow at mankind's selfishness and ingratitude to God).

To me, the image of Mary's heart in pain is symbolic of God's sorrow for all his children who are being crucified—from the starving children of North Korea and southern Sudan to the lonely heart of a teenager contemplating suicide. Mary's heart reminds us that, although we may not be suffering ourselves, many are, and they need our heartfelt prayers and support.

What does it mean to be "devoted" to the Immaculate Heart? Devotion doesn't mean we "worship" Mary as an idol. In both Eastern and Western spiritual traditions, devotion is a spiritual interchange, a transfer of energy, an empowerment.

When we place our attention on Mary (or another spiritual being), we create a figure-eight flow from our heart to their heart. We send our love to Mary, and on the return current she sends back to us, and to those in need, a charge of spiritual energy. That spiritual charge strengthens our heart so that we are better able to strengthen, comfort and uplift others.

Mary said in one of her messages through the Medjugorje seers, "I ask you to give me your heart so that I may change it and your heart may become like mine."[3] Through devotion to the heart of a saint or ascended master—whether it is the heart of Mary or Jesus, Gautama Buddha, Padma Sambhava or Kuan Yin—we create a sacred tie to heaven, a lifeline that can pull us through the trials of personal and world karma. In other messages through the seers, Mary explained:

> I am calling you to love.... Today I invite you to start working on your hearts.... Clean your hearts with love.... In the power of love you can do even those things that seem impossible to you.[4]

Expanding the Flame in Your Heart

When God created us, he placed a spiritual flame in our heart. That flame is the part of you that is divine. Christian mystics call this flame the divine spark, Kabbalists refer to it as the neshamah, and Hindus honor it as the Atman.

As we progress on our spiritual journey, we expand and intensify that heart flame. Intensifying the light in your heart is one way you can help neutralize the negative portents of prophecy; for as spiritual light intensifies, it disperses the darkness. And darkness cannot exist where there is light.

Why do we need someone like Mother Mary to help us develop our heart? It's the same reason we go to a heart specialist or an architect or an expert in any field, except in this case it's spiritual expertise we're looking for.

Sometimes, because of past traumas or pain, we have shut down portions of our heart. It often takes an "expert" to help us reopen the doors of our heart. When we engage in a figure-eight flow with Mary's Immaculate Heart, we can receive tremendous healing as our spiritual arteries are cleared of deep-seated or repressed anger, resentment or fear. The reason this is so important is that when our heart is cleared and strengthened, we are capable of nurturing and upholding many, many others with the light of our heart.

Another benefit of devotion to Mary's heart is that she can help us find our way in life because she holds for us the "immaculate," or pure, image of our soul—the divine image in which God created us. She sees the grand design behind our life and like a mother, she believes that we can fulfill our highest potential.

We are practicing devotion to the Immaculate Heart as we connect with Mary through her rosary and as we give affirmations like "In the Immaculate Heart of Mary, I trust!" or "I AM the Light of the Heart" (see pages 345, 361–71). When we say, "In the Immaculate Heart of Mary, I trust," we are affirming "Mary is here with me. She is taking care of me. I turn over my burdens to her and I place my total trust in her because I know that she will watch over me."

As you give affirmations and prayers to Mary, you can visualize light flowing from your heart to Mary's heart and from her heart back to yours. You can visualize her heart as it is traditionally portrayed in statues of the Blessed Mother or you can see it as a beautiful, glistening diamond, reflecting God's light and deflecting darkness.

Paying Off Karmic Debts

The third step of Mary's plan to achieve world peace is penance. What in Christian terms is called "penance" is simply making amends for our misdeeds, or our past negative karma—paying off our karmic debts. Penance is accepting responsibility for our actions and not blaming others for the circumstances of our lives. It is learning to take positive action instead of seeing ourselves as victims.

Francisco, one of the children Mary appeared to at Fátima, keenly felt the burdens that mankind place upon God and each other, and he clearly saw the need for making amends. One day his friends asked him, "What are you doing kneeling for such a long time?" The little child, who would recite several rosaries each day, replied that he was thinking of

God, who was so sad. "Oh, how I wish I could console him!" Francisco lamented. On another occasion, he said, "I love the Good God so much! But how sad he is on account of so many sins! Oh, we must not sin again."[5]

How can we fulfill Mary's request for "penance," for balancing our karmic debts? Whenever possible, we should of course try to make things right with the very people we have harmed in any way. We can also balance karma when we perform our daily work with love and when we volunteer to serve others who are less fortunate than we are.

In order to mitigate the impact of the returning karma prophesied for our time, it will take an accelerated form of "penance"—coupling good works with prayers, especially prayers that call forth the violet flame. A good starting point is to ask for forgiveness for yourself and for those who may have harmed you.

Through your prayers, you can send the violet flame of forgiveness to everyone you have ever wronged and everyone who has ever wronged you (see pages 341–42). Then you can expand your prayers and send the violet flame to any and all who are burdened. By giving violet-flame prayers, not only are you balancing your own karmic debts but you are also serving your fellowman.

Turning Challenges into Opportunities

When the Angel of Peace appeared to the three children at Fátima, he asked them to offer prayers and sacrifices to God on behalf of others. When Lucia asked, "How are we to make sacrifices?" the angel answered: "Make of everything you can a sacrifice and offer it to God as an act of reparation for the sins by which he is offended.... You will thus draw down peace upon your country."[6] In less conventional terms, this means turning your challenges into opportunities.

If something goes wrong in our lives, we often wonder why. Why me? Is it my karma or bad luck or just someone on a power trip taking me for a ride? Adversity may very well be the result of our karma. It can also be God testing us. Or it can be an invitation to turn a challenge into an opportunity and offer a sacrifice.

When we're going through something we don't like, when we're faced with doing something we would rather not do, think of the angel's words: "Make of everything you can a sacrifice and offer it to God." We can perform the works we do with a prayer in our heart: "I do this joyously and I offer it as a sacrifice for those who know not the way to go. Angels of light, cut them free from all negative influences that would cause them to harm others."

Over the years, Mother Mary has come to Mark Prophet and me with messages to comfort and enlighten spiritual seekers of all paths. She wants us all to know that there are *spiritual* solutions to our personal problems and to the problems of the world. I have excerpted below some of her most important teachings on prophecy, the power of prayer and the rosary, and how devotion to her heart can empower us.

Averting Prophecy

You have wondered why the ascended masters have not spelled out their prophecies more specifically. It is for the same reason that these have been told in secret, in part, to these children [at Fátima and Medjugorje]. Beloved, we never give the fullness of the vision of what karma could bring until almost the very hour of it, because until that time we are kneeling before the throne of the Father begging intercession and dispensation.

O beloved, realize, until the right hand of God descends, until the last grain of opportunity in the hourglass descends, there is opportunity, there is dispensation abundant for the world to be raised up, for all to change in the twinkling of the eye....

It is untold and unspoken as to that which could come upon the earth unless there be...

a tremendous increase in those who give the violet-flame decrees.   (May 11, 1987)

Prepare for the morrow and transmute your yesterdays lest they besmirch your tomorrows with those footprints of a past karma that will trip your soul and even shorten your life span if you are not careful. . . .

Establish a profound peace in God. Be not moved whatever is the next turn of events in your life. Hold fast to me.

I am a Mother of the seas and of the land and of the air. I am a Mother in the fire and the heart of the nucleus of the atom. . . . I give my very heart to forestall those certain conditions of karma that could descend.

They have been mitigated; and where they have not been mitigated, they have been simply held back. This has been because there are still those in the earth who decree, there are still those who invoke the violet flame.   (Aug. 22, 1992)

Empowerment through Prayer and the Rosary

I live with the Fátima prophecy. I live with its message. And I go from door to door and heart to heart knocking, asking for those who will come and pray with me—pray the violet flame or the rosary or the calls to Archangel Michael. But above all, pray.

For by thy prayer is the open door extended, and the angels come stepping through the veil to prevent disaster and calamity.   (Dec. 9, 1984)

We are divine helpers, able to help you, then, to bear the burden that so suddenly and sometimes, as it were, cruelly does come upon you. With violet flame and healing ray, my angels infuse you with a new life and strength.... So shall your strength be if you will but remember to connect with my heart in the rosary.   (Oct. 31, 1987)

Blessed ones, may I tell you, then, the scientific explanation of the prayer of the rosary and all decrees? It is a building up of light in the body, that you yourselves might deflect, as one mystical body of God, the oncoming darkness.

If a few men in a house in Japan could emerge whole after a nuclear holocaust, will you not, then, place your faith in the Divine Mother, in my intercession and in Almighty God first and foremost and always? Will you not understand that daily you need to be buoyed up in this spiritual light and flame?   (May 11, 1987)

I will never leave you who give that rosary each day. I cannot leave, for you by your devotion have established my presence around you. (Oct. 10, 1992)

I have presented myself to children always to teach them to pray and to pray the rosary, for in the rosary there is truly the raising up of the light of the Divine Mother. And where all else does fail, it is truly the Mother light that retains hope in the being and the soul and the consciousness of the individual. Blessed hearts, the Fátima message has not changed. You must understand this.

(March 1, 1988)

Measure for measure as you give, I give of myself to you and to millions whom I can reach through your heart when you regularly give the rosary.

(Aug. 22, 1992)

I am the Queen of Angels and in that office I may accord you a special grace or dispensation. I ask you to think about this... and then come to a conclusion as to what special grace you might ask of me....

Pursue the rosaries.... And when you come to knock on the door of my heart for a grace, you shall ask for a grace, I trust, that shall enable you to become who you are, to fulfill your mission and to serve others. (Aug. 22, 1992)

The Immaculate Heart Can Solve Knotty Problems

When there is no answer or solution (or decision forthcoming) to a particular knotty problem on the world scene, at home or in the church, I ask you to call to my heart. For my Immaculate Heart does hold the original blueprint for every event and eventuality that could come forth out of the creation of God. (April 21, 1987)

The Father did send me as a mediatrix of the divine wholeness. And as I have been allowed to come nearer to earth, even to the point where my tears are seen on my statues and images,[7] you may understand that truly through my heart you may achieve a daily oneness with your Christ Self [Higher Self]....

But I tell you, the power of the salutation to me "Hail, Mary! Hail, Ma-Ray!" and the mantra "In the Immaculate Heart of Mary, I trust!" is great. These, combined with the science of the spoken Word, the exercise thereof in the calling forth of the violet flame of the Holy Spirit, do so enhance your ability to maintain and strengthen the tie to my heart, and thus the tie to your [Higher] Self. Know, beloved, that my mission twenty-four hours a day is to restore to the child of God's heart that oneness that is so needed....

Blessed are ye who have a momentum...on prayer and service and in the things of God, for it is your momentum that will multiply again and again your daily prayers. (Oct. 11, 1988)

Where I weep, I weep for many reasons. I weep for ignorance. I weep for hardness of heart.... For I bear the Immaculate Heart for all religions and for all peoples....

I weep for those who do not even have the enlightenment or the love to give the rosary in the understanding of the mighty grid of light that is formed around them and the planet by the giving of the rosary—and that is reinforced each time they give it.   (Aug. 22, 1992)

Know that in the moments that you recite the rosary undisturbed, unmoved and in attunement with my Immaculate Heart, I may enter and become one with you and perform for you necessities of the hour, healing with direction and guidance and comfort for your hour of trial.

(Oct. 10, 1992)

Peace in the Heart Can Deflect War

It is the living flame of peace in your hearts and the hearts of all those who have been converted by my appearances that shall deflect war, even as a diamond heart does deflect it.   (May 11, 1987)

I pledge to you my heart, beloved. And I ask you if you might not also give your heart for the tipping of the balance in favor of light. May it count and be a compensation for all peoples of this nation. Overflowing the bounds of the nation, let it then be for the contacting of all hearts of light.

(Oct. 31, 1987)

When all else fails, beloved, it is the fire of the heart that will see you through. Therefore increase it while there is peace in the world, while you have a nation where you are not besieged either by famine or by war or the brutalities that you are seeing in Sarajevo. Blessed ones, these conditions in the earth are only a foreshadowing of the prophecies I have given. (Aug. 22, 1992)

God Is above Religion

Spirit is one.... Let the temples of individual lives, the temples of the world, and the varying religions of the world learn to understand this cardinal truth that they may cease in their warrings and begin to express universal compassion. (Sept. 3, 1972)

Above all, men should understand and apply the law of brotherhood and not be so hasty in their judgments of one another. For in many cases, right when we have sought to establish a very special assistance to one whose prayers evoked that assistance, his own dogmatism and loyalty to traditional concepts have become the enemy of all truth, barring him from receiving our intercession....

It is almost as though men themselves had created the religious tenets to which they adhere and, by and by, their loyalty to their own beliefs transcends their loyalty to God. But God is above mankind's religion.   (July 30, 1972)

The greatest of tragedies of life have arisen from those dogmas that through the years have aborted mankind's true sense of Reality—ideas, for example, that create feelings of distrust, doubt and fear....

When I consider the number of wars that have been fought and the conflicts that have been engaged in by mortal men in defense of political or religious ideals, I pray that more men and women will develop that strength of character which will afford them a greater degree of tolerance for one another's views and their right to hold them and thus bring about a state of peace on earth with good will to all.   (Sept. 24, 1972)

Meet the Human Need with Divine Love

I now make a plea for the avoidance of harshness in human life. How much suffering there is in the world order because of human selfishness and a lack of understanding between people! And, O mankind of earth, how much suffering occurs each day in the various countries of the world simply because of carelessness and human cruelty.

If individuals only knew the law [of karma]! For it is impossible to do harm to anyone without receiving the last jot and tittle of recompense, whether in this world or in the world to come. It is folly to think that men will escape the result of their own acts. In accordance with the consistency of cosmic law, it is ever true that as men sow, so shall they reap....

I make an impassioned plea to humanity, before it is too late and the karmic vials are poured out upon the earth, to seek to alleviate harshness, to repudiate it in all of its forms by the action of their thoughts powerfully centered in God. For man's inhumanity to man and his failure to meet the human need with divine love, whenever and wherever it appears, are often the result of hardness of heart....

Within you, each one, is light.   (Sept. 10, 1972)

Take My Hand

I am not only your Mother but your very personal friend. I ask you to take my hand, to take me to your home, to accept me as your friend, not as a remote deity, an icon or an object of irreverence, but simply as the handmaid of the Lord. Whose Lord? Your Lord.

I am the servant of the Lord who lives within you. I am one with whom you can be comfortable. I will sit at your kitchen table and have a cup of tea with you. I will receive whatever offering is precious to you and take it to my heart and give it back to you with the full consecration of my love.

I will help you in your daily tasks. Ask me for assistance in your problems, how to do this or that, and I will apply all that I have in my causal body of the understanding of science, technology, order, organization, administration, the managing of your household accounts, your supply, what you need for the elevation of your temple as healing methods....

Now won't you take me to your heart and talk to me, for so often I would befriend you but I am neglected and I feel that you do not want me in your house. And so I leave and go down the street, and I play with the little children. They are always very happy to have me come, for they know me one and all for I have been their sponsor at the hour of birth....

And so the little tiny ones jump with glee as I come. They laugh and they laugh when I swing with them. And when they see me on the seesaw with them, balancing three or five, they poke fun at me in my garments, jumping rope and doing all sorts of games with them. Do you know how few adults do play with children in the true spirit of childhood and innocence?

I am your friend and the friend of every head of state, every member of Congress and those who are seized with their self-importance. Beloved ones, I have the solution to many problems. If someone would but ask, I would tell them. Perhaps you should ask for your president, for his cabinet and all the rest. For so many of your representatives have been divested of the intercession of the... Mother because their religion does not partake of the Motherhood of God.

Truly many are in despair, knowing not how the problems of this nation will be resolved. And the more problems that come, the more problems are used as solutions to problems. And as you well know, one problem will not solve another; another error will not eliminate a former error.

(Dec. 31, 1977)

Let the Barriers Go Down

Beloved ones, I am very much the woman of the hour and I desire to teach you how to... release the energies of God for the resolution of every area of life. Now let us see how many of you will have a more real appreciation of my service and a sense that I am truly one like you, very much like you, in my evolution....

Whether you come with a face of Tibet or China or India or Africa or of America, may you be blessed with the understanding that all of the hosts of light are your friends, that the saints of every religion are the friend of the worshipers of God in every faith. This is my desire and I say, let the barriers go down. I raise my right hand and I say, Let the barriers go down. (Dec. 31, 1977)

11 Saint Germain & the Thread of Prophecy

*Something deeply hidden had to be
behind things.* —ALBERT EINSTEIN

The end of the eighteenth century marked the end of an old order in France. And one man was trying to make the transition as smooth as possible. He was the Comte de St. Germain, known throughout Europe as the "Wonderman."

His feats are exclamation points across the diaries of the eighteenth-century greats. He dazzled the aristocracy and the royal courts with youth potions, jewels and magical feats to engage their attention for a more serious purpose: to warn them of the impending revolution and the bloodbath that would follow. At the same time, he used his powers to expand scientific knowledge.

He is mentioned in the letters of Frederick the Great, Voltaire, Horace Walpole and Casanova, and even appears in the newspapers of the day—*The London Chronicle* of June 1760, the Florentine paper *Le notizie del Mondo* of July 1770, and the *Gazette of the Netherlands*.

He enjoyed the long-standing trust of those he dealt with at court and was entrusted with the state secrets of several countries. He was sent on negotiating missions by Louis XV, one of the first to practice secret diplomacy. The archives of France contain evidence that English, Dutch and Prussian statesmen of his time regarded the count as an authority in many fields.

In the court memoirs of Madame de Pompadour, Prince Karl of Hesse and Madame d'Adhémar, he is remembered as *l'homme extraordinaire*. Described as slim but well-proportioned, of medium height and with pleasant features, he had fascinating eyes that captivated the observing who chanced to study them.

The Man Who Would Not Die

One of the most remarkable things about the count was that he did not seem to age. In 1767, the Countess de Georgy asked him, "Will you have the kindness to tell me, whether your father was in Venice about the year 1710?"

"No, Madame," replied the count quite unconcerned, "it is very much longer since I lost my father; but I myself was living in Venice at the end of the last and the beginning of this century; I had the honour to pay you court then..."

"Forgive me, but that is impossible; the Comte de St. Germain I knew in those days was at least 45 years old, and you, at the outside, are that age at present."

"Madame," replied the count smiling, "I am very old."

"But then you must be nearly 100 years old."

"That is not impossible," Saint Germain replied.

In 1789, Madame d'Adhémar said after meeting him, "It was himself in person... Yes! with the same countenance as in 1760, while mine was covered with furrows and marks of decrepitude."[1]

The count's birth, death and true identity are shrouded in mystery. He was admired as a great philosopher, diplomat, scientist, healer, artist and musician. He knew history so well that it would seem he had actually experienced the events he related. Madame de Pompadour, Louis XV's influential mistress, recalled that "sometimes he recounted anecdotes of the court of the Valois [French royal house of 1328 to 1589] or of princes still more remote, with such precise accuracy in every detail as almost to create the illusion that he had been an eyewitness to what he narrated."

The Wonderman of Europe

The count's knowledge extended not only back in time but also around the globe. "He had traveled the whole world over," de Pompadour wrote, "and the king lent a willing ear to the narratives of his voyages over Asia and Africa, and to his tales about the courts of Russia, Turkey and Austria."

He spoke at least twelve languages so fluently that everywhere he went he was accepted as a native. These included French, German, English, Italian, Spanish, Portuguese, Russian and Eastern languages. "The learned and the oriental scholars have proved the knowledge of the Count St. Germain," wrote a countess at Louis XV's court. "The former found him more apt in the languages of Homer and Virgil than themselves; with the latter he spoke Sanskrit, Chinese, Arabic in such a manner as to show them that he had made some lengthy stay in Asia."

He was with General Clive in India in 1755, where he said he learned to melt jewels. At the court of the Shah of Persia from 1737 to 1742,

The Comte de St. Germain

Monsieur de Saint Germain exhibited his skill at precipitating and perfecting precious gems, particularly diamonds.

The count also traveled to Japan, as he told Madame d'Adhémar. There is no telling where else he visited, for he would appear and reappear unpredictably all over Europe. Yet there was a purpose behind all that the Wonderman did. And his wonders went far beyond mere genius.

He was skilled in healing and the use of medicinal herbs. Some have speculated that it was Saint Germain's use of herbs combined with his simple eating habits that prolonged his life. Prince Karl of Hesse wrote, "He thoroughly understood herbs and plants, and had invented the medicines of which he constantly made use, and which prolonged his life and health."

The count was a virtuoso on both the piano and violin as well as an accomplished painter, poet and artisan. Wherever he traveled, he was welcomed as scholar, statesman and raconteur. He formed secret societies, was a leading figure in the Rosicrucians, Freemasons and Knights Templar of the period, and penned the occult classic *The Most Holy Trinosophia,* using a mixture of modern languages and ancient hieroglyphics.

A Master Alchemist

Monsieur de Saint Germain never confirmed or denied anything that was said about him. Instead, he would respond with a smile or a studied evasiveness. His skill as an alchemist was praised by Louis XV, who provided him a laboratory and residence at the royal castle of Chambord. And his alchemical demonstrations were nothing short of miraculous according to his chroniclers.

The count was not only an alchemist, but an Eastern adept, displaying yogic behavior, meditating in the lotus posture and calming animals by his fiery spirit. One Dutch admirer, J. van Sypesteyn, wrote, "Sometimes he fell into a trance, and when he again recovered, he said he had passed the time while he lay unconscious in far-off lands; sometimes he disappeared for a considerable time, then suddenly reappeared, and let it be understood that he had been in another world in communication with the dead."

Prince Karl of Hesse described him as "the friend of humanity, wishing for money only that he might give to the poor; a friend to animals, his heart was concerned only with the happiness of others."

"Wherever he was personally known he left a favourable impression behind, and the remembrance of many good and sometimes of many noble deeds. Many a poor father of a family, many a charitable institution, was helped by him in secret," van Sypesteyn wrote.

The Inevitable Passing of the Old Order

Why all of the extravaganza at court? What was Saint Germain trying to prove? He was trying, precisely—with wit and humor and his prophetic, masterful presence—to galvanize an age in the face of the inevitable passing of the old order. His plan of action was to establish a United States of Europe—before the pulling of the ripcord of the bloody French Revolution should leave nothing bad or good of the royal houses of Europe.

Another of Saint Germain's aims was to accelerate the progress of science and technology so that mankind could have time to pursue a greater spiritual awareness. At times he played the part of patron saint of the Industrial Revolution.

Count Karl Cobenzl witnessed his development of mass-production techniques. Among them were bleaching flax to look like Italian silk, dyeing and preparing skins "which surpassed all the moroccos in the world, and the most perfect tanning; the dyeing of silks, carried to a perfection hitherto unknown; the like dyeing of woollens; the dyeing of wood in the most brilliant colours penetrating through and through... with the commonest ingredients, and consequently at a very moderate price."

The monarchs, while in admiration of his miraculous accomplishments, pronounced them "interesting." Always willing to be entertained by him, they were not easily prodded into action. When it came to taking his advice, they politely ignored him; and their ministers, jealous to the quick, despised him.

Seeking a smooth transition from the monarchy to a new form of government, Saint Germain tried to warn Louis XVI and Marie Antoinette that a revolution was festering. Unfortunately, his efforts were thwarted. Monsieur de Saint Germain continued to write letters to the queen, warning of impending debacle, but once the crisis had reached a certain point there was nothing he could do to turn back the revolution that had been building.

The lesson is wisely and painfully learned: a sage of great mastery, having only the best of intentions and the solution to global problems and the rise and fall of nations, must bow to the free will of mortals. He may advise, but not command; and when ignored, he is obliged to withdraw.

As his last hope for creating a united community in Europe, Saint Germain backed Napoleon. Le Petit Caporal took Saint Germain's power, but not his advice, and sought to use it in self-gain, exceeding the master's instructions. Saint Germain once again was forced to withdraw, leaving the ambitious and foolhardy Napoleon to his Waterloo.

A New Experiment in Freedom

In his devotion to the cause of world freedom, Saint Germain had been working diligently on many fronts. "Having failed in securing the attention of the Court of France and others of the crowned heads of Europe," he said, "I turned myself to the perfectionment of mankind at large.

"I recognized that there were many who, hungering and thirsting after righteousness, would indeed be filled with the concept of a perfect union which would inspire them to take dominion over the New World and create a Union among the sovereign states. Thus the United States was born as a child of my heart and the American Revolution was the means of bringing freedom in all of its glory into manifestation from the East unto the West."

Even before the denouement in France, Saint Germain was busy forming a more perfect union out of the Thirteen Colonies. According to tradition, on July 4, 1776, he inspired upon one of the signers of the Declaration of Independence an impassioned speech urging them to "Sign that document!"

Saint Germain reappeared in the latter nineteenth century to assist the Masters M. (El Morya), K.H. (Koot Hoomi), and Serapis Bey in the found-ing of the Theosophical Society through Helena Blavatsky. His name, literally Sanctus Germanus, means simply "holy brother."

In the 1930s, Saint Germain contacted Guy and Edna Ballard and gave them the teachings they recorded in the books *Unveiled Mysteries, The Magic Presence* and the *I AM Discourses*. In 1958, Saint Germain began working with Mark L. Prophet through The Summit Lighthouse to publish the on-going teachings of the ascended masters on practical spirituality.

Today Saint Germain comes to the fore as the sponsor of the Aquarian age. He played many roles in many lifetimes, as we all have. The thread that runs through them all is the thread of prophecy.

Saint Germain was always a visionary who ex-tolled and exemplified freedom of the mind and spirit. He has ingeniously sought to protect our in-alienable right to live life according to our highest conception of God. For he has said that no right, however basic, can long be secure without the underpinning of the spirituality that instills a com-passionate use of that right.

To better understand the mission of this master, let us look at some of his past incarnations.

A Warning Heeded and a Prophecy Averted

As the eleventh-century prophet Samuel, the last and greatest of the judges of the twelve tribes of Israel, Saint Germain sought to liberate the Israelites from bondage to the corrupt priests, the sons of Eli and the Philistines. In those days, the judges of Israel did more than settle disputes. Some were charismatic leaders who were thought to have direct access to God, and they rallied the tribes of Israel against oppressors.

Samuel delivered to the recalcitrant Israelites a prophecy parallel to his modern-day messages—both inextricably linked with karma and free will. He told them that if they did not stop worshiping "strange gods" instead of the one true God, they would be defeated. "If you do return to the Lord with all your hearts, then put away the strange gods and Ashtaroth from among you," Samuel chided them. "Direct your heart to the Lord and serve him only, and he will deliver you out of the hand of the Philistines."

The prophet's exhortation stirred the entire nation to give up their false gods and renew their spirituality. With Samuel leading them, all the Israelites gathered together, fasted and reconsecrated themselves to God. They admitted that they had fallen short of the mark, and they begged Samuel to plead with God on their behalf to save them from their enemy. As a result of their turning back to God and Samuel's prayers, "the Philistines were subdued and did not again enter the territory of Israel."[2]

Like the story of Ninevah recorded in the Book of Jonah, this is an important lesson that prophecy is not set in stone. It shows us that a people who heed the word of the prophets and reaffirm their spiritual orientation can be spared the consequences of their karma.

When Samuel grew old, the Israelites demanded a king, "like all the nations." He warned them that a king would become a tyrant and usurp their freedoms, but to no avail. Bowing to their free will, God directed Samuel to appoint a king. "They have not rejected thee," God told Samuel, "but they have rejected me, that I should not reign over them."[3] The prophet obeyed and anointed Saul king. Later, when Saul disobeyed God, Samuel freed the people from his tyranny by anointing David as their new king.

A Prophetic Voice in a Medieval Wilderness

In the thirteenth century, Saint Germain was embodied as Roger Bacon, possibly the most gifted man of that century. Viewed as the forerunner of modern science, his was the voice of one crying in the intellectual and scientific wilderness that was medieval Britain. In an era in which either theology or logic or both dictated the parameters of science, he promoted the experimental method, declared his belief that the world was round, and castigated the scholars and scientists of his day for their narrow-mindedness.

He was also a prophet of modern technology. He predicted the hot-air balloon, a flying machine, spectacles, the telescope, microscope, elevator, and mechanically propelled ships and carriages—and wrote of them as if he had actually seen them. Bacon was also the first Westerner to write down the exact directions for making gunpowder, but he kept the formula a secret lest it be used to harm anyone.

From whence did Bacon believe he derived his amazing awareness? "True knowledge stems not from the authority of others, nor from a blind allegiance to antiquated dogmas," he said. His biographers write that he believed knowledge "is a highly personal experience—a light that is communicated only to the innermost privacy of the individual through the impartial channels of all knowledge and of all thought."[4]

Experiments on the Magnetic Forces of Love

Bacon, who had been a lecturer at Oxford and the University of Paris, determined to seek and find his science in his religion. Entering the Franciscan Order of Friars Minor, he said, "I will conduct my experiments on the magnetic forces of the lodestone at the selfsame shrine where my fellow-scientist, St. Francis, performed his experiments on the magnetic forces of love."[5]

The friar's scientific and philosophical world view, his bold attacks on the theologians of his day, and his study of alchemy, astrology and magic led to charges of "heresies and novelties," for which he was imprisoned in 1278 by his fellow Franciscans. They kept him in solitary confinement for fourteen years, releasing him only shortly before his death. Although the clock of this life was run out, his body broken, he knew that his efforts would not be without impact on the future.

The following prophecy which he gave his students shows the grand and revolutionary ideals of the indomitable spirit of this living flame of freedom —the immortal spokesman for our scientific, religious and political liberties:

> I believe that humanity shall accept as an axiom for its conduct the principle for which I have laid down my life—the right to investigate. It is the credo of free men—this opportunity to try, this privilege to err, this courage to experiment anew.
>
> We scientists of the human spirit shall experiment, experiment, ever experiment. Through centuries of trial and error, through agonies of research

... let us experiment with laws and customs, with money systems and governments, until we chart the one true course—until we find the majesty of our proper orbit as the planets above have found theirs. ... And then at last we shall move all together in the harmony of our spheres under the great impulse of a single creation—one unity, one system, one design.[6]

Setting the Stage

As Francis Bacon (1561–1626), the greatest mind the West has ever produced, Saint Germain's manifold achievements in every field catapulted the world into a stage set for the children of Aquarius. In this life he was free to carry to its conclusion the work he had begun as Roger Bacon.

Scholars have noted the similarities between the thoughts of the two philosophers and even between Roger's *Opus Majus* and Francis' *De Augmentis* and *Novum Organum*. This is even more astounding because Roger's *Opus* was never published in his lifetime. It fell into oblivion, and did not appear in print until more than a century after Francis' *Novum Organum* and *De Augmentis*.

Francis Bacon is known as the father of inductive reasoning and the scientific method which, more than any other contributions, are responsible for the age of technology in which we now live. He foreknew that only applied science could free the masses from human misery and the drudgery of sheer survival in order that they might seek a higher spirituality they once knew.

Universal Enlightenment

His next step was to be nothing less bold than universal enlightenment. "The Great Instauration" (restoration after decay, lapse, or dilapidation) was his formula to change "the whole wide world." First conceived when Bacon was a boy of 12 or 13 and later crystallized in 1607 in his book by the same name, it did indeed launch the English Renaissance with the help of Francis' tender, caring person.

Over the years, he gathered around himself a group of luminaries who were responsible among other things for almost all of the Elizabethan literature—Ben Jonson, John Davies, George Herbert, John Selden, Edmund Spenser, Sir Walter Raleigh, Gabriel Harvey, Robert Greene, Sir Philip Sidney, Christopher Marlowe, John Lyly, George Peele, and Lancelot Andrewes.

Some of these were part of a "secret society" that Francis had formed with his brother, Anthony, when the two were law students at Gray's Inn. This fledgling group, called the Knights of the Helmet, had as its goal the advancement of learning by expanding

the English language and by creating a new literature written not in Latin but in words that English-
men could understand.

Francis also organized the translation of the
King James Version of the Bible, determined that the
common people should have the benefit of reading
the scriptures for themselves. Some even claim,
based on ciphers embedded in the type of the original printings of the Shakespearean Folios, that Francis Bacon was the real author of the plays attributed
to the actor from the village of Stratford-on-Avon.[7]

Bacon was also behind many of the political
ideas on which Western civilization is based. Thomas
Hobbes, John Locke and Jeremy Bentham took
Bacon as their ideological starting point. His revolutionary principles are the engine that has driven
our nation. They are the very essence of the can-do
spirit. "Men are not animals erect," Bacon averred,
"but immortal Gods. The Creator has given us souls
equal to all the world, and yet satiable not even
with a world."[8]

Francis Bacon promoted the colonization of the
New World, for he knew that it was there that his
ideas could take deepest root and come to fullest
flower. He convinced James I to charter Newfound-
land and was an officer in the Virginia Company,
which sponsored the settlement of Jamestown,

England's first permanent colony in America. He also founded Freemasonry, dedicated to the freedom and enlightenment of mankind, whose members played a large part in founding the new nation.

After being accused of bribery on trumped-up charges, Bacon resigned his seal of office. He died a persecuted man who had never been fully recognized for his many talents. Yet he had triumphed over circumstances that would have destroyed lesser men. For him, these challenges proved the making of an ascended master.

On May 1, 1684, Saint Germain reunited with God through the ritual of the ascension and became an ascended master. Desiring above all else to liberate God's people, Saint Germain sought a dispensation from God to return to earth in a physical body. Such a request is rarely approved, but it was granted and he reappeared as the Comte de St. Germain.

Champion of Soul Liberation

The advances Saint Germain has made in education, spirituality, science and government over the centuries were laying the foundation for Aquarius. Saint Germain is the champion par excellence of the path of our soul liberation. Throughout his embodiments, his soul has been internalizing the inner light of freedom. His spiritual attainment and soul resonance with the sacred quality of freedom, his genuine love for humanity and deep commitment to safeguarding our freedom to pursue our chosen path has earned him the role of sponsor of the Aquarian age.

The age of Aquarius is an age when we are meant to refine our understanding of freedom and love and express these qualities for the full flowering of our soul. Saint Germain, the master alchemist, teaches us how to master the energies of love and how to become alchemists ourselves as we perform our experiments in self-transformation. He is the champion of our souls' right to become who we really are.

I had my first experience with Saint Germain in this life when I was eighteen. I opened an old book on the ascended masters that had been in my parents' library and I found myself face to face with his picture. I looked into his eyes and recognized him as an old, old friend. It changed my life. I said to myself, "I have to find this master."

In April 1961, I attended a meeting of The Summit Lighthouse in Boston, where I met its leader, Mark L. Prophet. Mark was dedicated to publishing the teachings of the ascended masters as their messenger, or spokesman. He would become both my teacher and my husband. Mark was the most spiritual man I have ever known. He was profoundly one with God, deeply compassionate and a wonderful tutor of my soul and the souls of many seekers.

Not long after I met Mark, I entered a period of rigorous spiritual training and in 1964, Saint Germain anointed me as a messenger. A messenger is both a spokesman and scribe for the "ascended masters," those who have mastered life on earth and attained reunion with God, ascending as Jesus did. Empowered by the Holy Spirit, I speak and write down their teachings.

Many Ways to Reach the Summit

There's an old Arab proverb, "God has given to every people a prophet in its own tongue." Out of his great love and compassion, God has always provided a messenger or a prophet who could convey his words to his children sojourning on earth in a way that they could understand. The role of that one is to teach, to warn, to comfort and to show the people how to attain union with God.

God spoke through the ancient prophets to guide and warn the Israelites. In the first century, Jesus sent his angel to the island of Patmos to give the Book of Revelation to John. The Buddhist adept Asanga received the direct teaching of the Bodhisattva Maitreya in the fourth century. In the seventh century, Archangel Gabriel revealed the words of the Koran to Mohammed. In the fourteenth century, God the Father dictated his teachings to Saint Catherine of Siena, and the Bodhisattva Manjushri taught Tsong Khapa, who went on to renew the course of Buddhism in Tibet.

Through his messengers in the various religions of the world, God unveils different aspects of himself so that the people of diverse cultures can understand—and assimilate—the different attributes of his divine personality. For there are many ways to climb to the summit of being, to reach the Universal Source. Each path offers a different perspective of the summit—a new way of understanding who God is and who you are.

Today God has sent his ascended masters to give prophecies and revelations to prepare us for the Aquarian age and to show us that we are destined to walk our own path of self-mastery. In this and the last century, the masters have given their teachings through Helena Blavatsky in the Theosophical Society, Mary Baker Eddy in the Christian Science movement, Guy and Edna Ballard in the I AM movement, and Nicholas and Helena Roerich in the Agni Yoga Society, among others. Most recently, the masters have been delivering their teachings through Mark L. Prophet and me.

To serve as a messenger is a great privilege and honor. It is a gift from God. A messenger of God's word is not a master but only the instrument of the master. Thus I see myself as the servant of the light of God within all people, no matter what spiritual path they are on.

The ascended masters present a path and a teaching that can help us become acquainted with our real self and develop a one-on-one relationship with God. They also teach us advanced spiritual techniques we can use to accelerate the power and love of our hearts for personal and world transformation. In the next chapter, we follow the thread of Saint Germain's prophecies for the Aquarian age and his formula for making it into a golden age.

12 Prophecy Is Not Set in Stone

*The future is called "perhaps," which
is the only possible thing to call the future.
And the important thing is not to allow
that to scare you.* —TENNESSEE WILLIAMS

With the true eye of a prophet, Saint Germain sees the future as unpredictable—unpredictable because moment by moment we are changing what the future will look like.

Saint Germain does not mince words. He sets before us the current reality. Then he shows us probabilities and possibilities so that we can choose wisely. He sees the potential for peace and enlightenment, the potential for decline and disintegration. He emphasizes that our daily choices and our concerted actions will have dramatic consequences. But whatever happens, he says, things will not remain as they are.

The messages a prophet brings are not confined to warnings. Contrary to popular belief, prophecy is not fortune telling, crystal-ball gazing or psychic prediction. Since prophecy can be revoked, a prophet not only speaks God's word, but must also compel his listeners to initiate a deep and enduring change of heart. As Paul wrote to the early Christians, prophecy is for edification, exhortation and comfort[1]—in other words, a prophet seeks to enlighten, to encourage and to console.

Saint Germain not only points the way to the goal, but he shows us how to get there. With love, determination and persistency, he gives the solution to our karmic dilemma: a high-frequency spiritual energy known as the violet flame. Saint Germain calls it "the cosmic eraser."

In Part II, "Spiritual Solutions," we explain how to apply the violet flame to personal and world conditions through prayer and meditation. In this chapter, we unfold Saint Germain's prophecies. We have also included a little-known vision that George Washington had while he was camped at Valley Forge during the winter of 1777.

Saint Germain

A Golden Age Is Not Guaranteed

Saint Germain tells us that the opening years of the new millennium are crucial because what we do now will reverberate for centuries:

> I have set before you certain portents of the current and upcoming astrology so that you might understand that just because the cosmic clock says we are entering the age of Aquarius does not guarantee that it shall be a golden age....
>
> You are on stage! And you will play your parts, as I have played my part (and many parts) on the world stage. Yes, today it is your choices—the choices that you make, beloved—that will determine the course of this civilization....
>
> I, then, would tell you that what you have heard in my prophecies...is but a mere portent of things to come. I would tell you that never in your history since you first placed your feet on this planet and on this soil have you had such a challenge as you now face and as you and your progeny will be facing in the next two hundred years.
>
> (March 2, 1996)

> There is a potential for absolute cataclysm and a potential for an absolute golden age. (April 7, 1996)

> My determination to have this victory is great and my vision is vast. May yours be the same. And

when it comes to bringing in the golden age, do not take no for an answer. If you must, knock upon the doors of heaven night and day for dispensations that will assist me in fulfilling the dream of heaven and earth to make the golden age of Aquarius a reality.   (March 2, 1996)

The Karmic Ledger

People ask, "Why are cataclysm and earth changes predicted?" They are predicted, beloved, because of mankind's unbalanced karma that has been on the ledger... for thousands upon thousands of years. Therefore Almighty God has spoken and has said to the mankind of earth: "Thus far and no farther!"   (March 2, 1996)

The sine wave of the ages continues regardless of the comings and goings of humanity. It is irrevocable. It can no more be stopped than the rising and the setting of the sun or the rotation of the earth around the sun....

In order for humanity to triumph over their returning negative karma that has been accumulating for 25,800 years, they must collectively row upstream, so to speak.

Yes, humanity must reverse the tide of their descending karma so that they might transmute that karma by their violet-flame decrees before it crystallizes in the physical octave. For once humanity's negative karma does crystallize in the earth, in the four lower bodies of the people and in all life, animate and inanimate, it will take a tremendous effort on the part of the enlightened ones of earth to purify the world of its human effluvia.

(March 2, 1996)

The Quickest Way to Balance Karmic Debts

Here Saint Germain explains that the violet flame can help us pay off outstanding karmic debts that we may not even realize we have:

Think, then, if unwittingly eight thousand years ago you were a part of a band of brigands, of evil souls who did nothing but torment life, destroy life. Think of this, beloved. Think if you were perhaps responsible for an entire nation to fall. Think if you were in these positions....

Perhaps you made an invention and that invention was detrimental to mankind, even without your intent. Think how many of mankind, then, may have suffered because of this invention, though you had good intentions. So you have karma with those who have been burdened....

The only way you could possibly balance your karma in this life would be through the amplification of your calls through a planetary system of the action of decrees to the violet flame. (Oct. 9, 1995)

As you invoke that violet flame by the power of the God within you, you shall see planetary change. I call for millions to join in the call to the violet flame...

I ask you to see how that violet flame going forth from you will help all whom you meet and will support your leaders to make right choices, will enlighten the populace so that they also may properly exercise their vote.   (April 27, 1991)

If you who know better do not engage in serious karma balancing, giving powerful fiats [short, dynamic commands or affirmations] to the violet flame for world transmutation, you could very well see come to pass that cataclysm that has been predicted for so long. And if it come to pass, the advances civilization has achieved to this hour could take thousands of years to regain, depending on the severity of earth changes. Continents could be severed and nations divided.

(March 2, 1996)

Be Not Lulled by the Heyday

Saint Germain gave the following message several months before the 1987 crash known as Black Monday, when the stock market tumbled 508 points, the largest percentage drop ever. Saint Germain still warns us not to be lulled by the heyday because economic downturns can come when we least expect them unless we do our spiritual work.

> Economic debacle is foreseen. Prepare. Setbacks will be sudden. Be not lulled by the heyday. Many Band-Aids upon the economy, the money system, the banking houses. These will not prevent the collapse of nations and banking houses built on sands of human greed, ambition and manipulation of the lifeblood of the people of God....
>
> The mitigating factor in economic debacle, in nuclear war, in plague untold and death is the nucleus of lightbearers and the quotient of sacred fire they invoke.... We have, then, a tripod of war, economic debacle and cataclysm. Any one of these could be sprung at any time.
>
> We are determined. You must be determined. When we do all in our power to assist you, you must appreciate how urgent is the moment and the hour—how great the need of response.
>
> (November 27, 1986)

Atlantis and Lemuria Revisited

Like Edgar Cayce, Saint Germain tells us that we face the same challenges that brought down the ancient civilizations of Atlantis and Lemuria—and the same opportunities to recapture the golden-age civilization they once knew.

Not once or twice but for many incarnations I walked the earth as you now do, confined to mortal frame and the limitations of dimensional existence. I was on Lemuria and I was on Atlantis. I have seen civilizations rise and fall. I have seen the undulations of consciousness as mankind have cycled from golden ages to primitive societies.

I have seen the choices and I have seen mankind by wrong choices squander the energies of a hundred thousand years of scientific advancement and even degrees of cosmic consciousness which transcend that which is attained by members of the most advanced religions of the day. (July 27, 1975)

Some of you have entered in to this materialistic civilization, and it has cost you. For you have been driven this way and that way, looking to outer things, forgetting that you once knew and tended the flame on the altar of the heart.   (July 4, 1996)

Alas, it is late in the centuries, and some of those who have come to be reborn here to build America in this century and the last have not fulfilled their reason for being. Some have entered into the same old [Atlantean] spirals of deception, the abuse of power and money, and have therefore turned around what might have been truly by this day a golden age in America.   (Oct. 14, 1991)

I remind you that certain karma of ancient Lemuria is upon most of the students who call themselves the avant-garde of the new age, who pursue a path that is above and apart from the orthodox traditions of the world's major religions.

Because you have had part in some of the negative karma of Lemuria, one and all wherever you live upon earth may contribute to the success of this violet flame....

You live in a moment, and it is a moment of cosmic history, when by the application of the violet-flame decrees you can eliminate much karma and therefore much misery in the future....

Many have studied in the violet-flame temples of Atlantis. Many knew the efficacy of this flame for the physical healing of the body and for the changing of world conditions. Now you are restored to that place where you can rise even higher in your application [of the violet flame].

(May 1, 1991)

Marvel not that many of you made scientific discoveries more than twelve thousand years ago on Atlantis, which you must once again bring forth in the age of Aquarius. Under my careful oversight, you will perfect these inventions. And if you freely lay them on the altar of humanity and thereby benefit the race, you may win your ascension at the conclusion of this life. (March 2, 1996)

Of a truth, I have been working toward the goal of raising the consciousness of the people of this hemisphere for tens of thousands of years.

Realize that I have been with you for a long, long time—going as far back as Atlantis and Lemuria. And we, together, have come to the nexus where the configurations of light and darkness allow our souls to pass through the eye of the needle and raise this civilization to forgotten heights of glory.   (March 10, 1996)

Prophecy Is Never Final

One of Saint Germain's great rallying cries is *Prophecy is never set in stone*. The master alchemist says that if we respond to the prophets' warnings and apply the spiritual solutions they place before us, calamity can be averted.

Jonah went to Nineveh and he warned the people that unless they would repent from their squandering of the life-force in the pleasure cult, calamity would ensue. Much to his disappointment, the people repented. They hearkened unto the voice of God through him and the city was spared.

And thus, Jonah complained to the Lord, "They will consider me a false prophet because the calamity did not come upon the city." Thus, God can spare the city, even as he can pass the resurrection flame through the withered gourd, to which the prophet may become attached.

Beloved ones, understand the meaning of this—that the prophecy that is written in Revelation and in the Old and New Testament, that is written in the very sands and in the ethers which may be perceived, is not final! This is my cry to the age!... Karma can be transmuted! (May 28, 1986)

See the handwriting on the wall: on schedule, the descending karma, the seven last plagues, the Four Horsemen—all delivering to the earth the mandate of personal and planetary karma. Yet God has already arranged ahead of time and from time immemorial for the staying of the hand of that darkness, for its transmutation by the light of the heart and by the sacred fire. (July 6, 1985)

The Few Can Make the Difference

What you can do to work planetary change is unlimited. I said it is unlimited! The infinite power of God is available to you, greater than all nuclear power or weapons.

This is not a theory or a metaphysical statement. It is a law that you can make physical by the spiritual fire merging in the chalice of being. May none ever be compelled to look back upon this century and say, "What might have been..." (Feb. 22, 1987)

What is noteworthy, beloved, is that in all areas of crisis and ultimate catastrophe, it has taken but a few lightbearers to save a situation and but a few spoilers to ruin all for the people. Thus understand that key figures play their parts this day, even as chessmen on the board of life.... Recognize that in you the light is a majority....

Your actions, choices, moves and decisions will truly affect the fate of earth and her destiny for centuries to come.   (October 21, 1987)

I charge you not to allow any condemnation upon you that would make you think, because you have this foible, this idiosyncrasy, this problem, that you simply don't count.... Well, I tell you, you do count!
                                        (July 4, 1996)

Get off of your couches!   (May 1, 1983)

A Friend on the Path

I took the name Saint Germain, for it means "holy brother." May you think of me always as your friend and brother on the path. And may you know that I may not enter your world to intercede for you unless you call my name in the name of God and ask.

Therefore, say it to me any hour of the day or night—*"In the name of Almighty God, Saint Germain, help me now!"* I promise you that an electronic presence of myself shall be at your side with the speed of light.

And if you desire to increase your capacity to receive my assistance, then take up the calls to the violet flame and see how your aura will actually turn a violet color....

O beloved, let me help you! Receive me now as your friend forever.   (Feb. 7, 1987)

I have come to claim your soul and the fires of your heart for the victory of the Aquarian age. I have set the pattern for your soul's initiation. I have come to be your teacher. And the word of the Lord has been given unto me in this age....

Now these are the words that I speak. I have a message. Give ear to me, children of the one God! It is a message of freedom, of opportunity to rise to be what in fact you, as the stars, are ordained to be. I will assist you to implement the divine plan of your life. I will come to you, and I will speak within your heart.   (July 27, 1975)

I am the guard of your soul's liberation in the age of Aquarius.   (Aug. 17, 1975)

Technology for Peace Not War

Saint Germain and other masters have sponsored the development of technology so that we could be free to spend more time on the development of our soul, the illumination of mankind, and the improvement of conditions on earth. Unfortunately, some have used this gift of science to increase materialism rather than spirituality.

Today the stakes are becoming higher than ever before. For instance, the same technology that can accelerate our power to network and communicate quickly—the Internet—can also be exploited for "information terrorism," the transfer of information about how to execute a terrorist campaign. As Isaac Asimov once said, "Our lifetime may be the last that will be lived out in a technological society." Here Saint Germain makes a plea that we use technology for peace not war:

> The developments that I have sponsored, beloved, for I am the sponsor of modern science, have truly been used to build a war machine without equal since the ancient days. Therefore, beloved, let that science be withdrawn from the movement for war and be applied to peace.
>
> Peace is the purpose of technology—and the growth of the human spirit. And where people make science their god, they have no recourse when those forces of darkness, more powerful than themselves, amalgamate and rise up.   (April 27, 1991)

This is our goal for you, beloved, that there should be war no more in the earth—no more war in your members or on the planetary body. You are moving toward that, beloved. May you attain it in this life so that those who come after you need not take a backward step. (July 4, 1998)

The Grand Opportunity of the 21st Century

In the following excerpts we can see that Saint Germain is not a prophet of doom and gloom. Although he is realistic about our challenges, his vision of the future is one of humanity moving into a golden age of enlightenment, peace and spiritual transcendence.

The twenty-first century will open the door for all to renew past ties, both positive and negative, so that all might greet their karma with this one and that one, balance the negatives, accentuate the positives and achieve the goal of absolute karmic freedom at the conclusion of this life.

This is indeed a goal worth striving for!

(March 2, 1996)

I see the dawn of a new day.... Magnificent beings of light ... are rooting for this victory. I say to you, make it happen. You have the ability.

Make it happen! Make it happen! Make it

happen! And we shall see what a world of a golden age shall dawn before us.   (April 7, 1996)

By your diligent application of the violet flame you can not only forestall cataclysm but also accelerate world enlightenment.   (March 2, 1996)

We see great progress in the world order; it is a progress of internal cycles. While we recognize that that which is unreal, that that which is of the dark...must be no more, must be bound and set aside, we see the strength of the green shoot.

(Jan. 1, 1984)

Remain calm and peaceful in your hearts and remember my words; for we look to the future and to the victory. We claim it! We expect it! We invoke it from our God! And we are here to help you.

May you maintain that stance of absolute conviction that your feet are firmly planted in this soil, that God has set you here for a destiny and not to lose all in this moment. God has sent you for a cosmic purpose. You have known it from your birth! I, Saint Germain, tell you that this is that cosmic purpose: It is the continuity of life that has the quality of the spiritual golden thread running through it, a spiritual quality.   (Oct. 8, 1989)

Aquarius Is an Age of Love

Let the tenderness of your hearts increase. Purify the heart and the heart chakra. Expand love! Give love! And see how your love joined with others' will establish the foundation of the age of Aquarius.

Aquarius is the age of freedom, but it is also the age of love. And that love personified in the people of earth gives us the wherewithal to carry the momentum of this civilization into new heights of attainment beyond their fondest dreams.

(March 23, 1996)

Love is the point of victory. It is the intense fire of the heart that can unite with every other fiery heart on earth through the power of meditation, that can unite with angelic hosts and ascended ones.

Yes, the fire of the heart, let it be developed! And may you never again have a vibration in your heart of hatred, of revenge, of nonmercy and of inattention to helpless life.   (April 27, 1991)

The Prophecy of the Seventh Root Race

If we could read the pages of the ancient and hidden history of the world, they would reveal the marvels of illustrious golden-age civilizations. Those who walked the earth in those days are known in esoteric tradition as members of the first three "root races."

A root race is a group of souls who embody together and who share a unique archetypal pattern and mission. The first root races lived in harmony with each other and with the laws of the universe. They expressed the highest potential of their souls, fulfilled their reason for being and reunited with God.

It was during the time of the fourth root race that the "fall" of Adam and Eve took place. These two souls were influenced by a fallen angel (represented in the Bible by the serpent) and subsequently left "paradise," a higher state of consciousness. Many others followed. Derailed from their spiritual path, they lost the vision of their quest for divine wholeness and created karma. Some have been reincarnating on earth to this day.

The souls of the fifth and sixth root races embodied into this imperfect world and they, too, became misguided, made karma, forgot their divine origins and lost sight of their purpose in life. Many members of the fifth and sixth root races are also in embodiment.

As a result of the unpredictable conditions on earth today, the souls of the next root race, the seventh, have not yet been allowed to embody, for it would jeopardize their spiritual development. Saint Germain says South America is destined to be the cradle for the unique, advanced souls of the seventh root race.

Saint Germain has given a number of prophecies about the seventh root race, explaining what we must do to prepare for these precious souls who can do so much to help us once again enter a golden-age culture. Some of his most recent teachings on this subject are excerpted below.

The Special Role of North and South America

The entire planet shall have the opportunity to bring in a golden age of Aquarius, but it is South America that God has chosen as the place that must be prepared for the incarnation of these holy innocents—souls whose precious feet have never touched the earth.

Yet, as I have said and as other ascended masters have said, this is a time when we must hold back even though we would move forward, for we cannot recommend that the souls of the seventh root race be born to mothers and fathers on this continent [South America] until the leadership of the nations with the support of their constituents will right the wrongs of society....

Think of it: these souls have no negative karma! And by and by, they will enter this civilization and set an example to all of what it means to excel. (March 4, 1996)

Elohim, who created the earth "in the beginning," have controlled earth changes throughout the ages as continents have risen and fallen according to mankind's karma. Through such earth changes, they have fashioned what you know today as the Western Hemisphere—stretching as it does from the North to the South Pole—to be isolated between the Atlantic and Pacific Oceans.

This was for a very good reason. It was in part to protect the golden-age civilization that I envisioned would one day thrive in the New World. The golden age, I believed, would see its beginnings in North and South America and then sweep the world around.   (March 7, 1996)

Care for the Children

Are not our lives, yours as well as ours, already filled with responsibilities? Indeed they are. And they always will be. Therefore I ask you to see what activities you can set aside so that you can make room in your lives for the larger issues, most importantly, bringing in the golden age of Aquarius....

See what steps you must take that are absolutely vital to your securing the spiritual victory of your soul and the souls of your children, your extended families and your nations....

Now ask yourself the following question: "What will I have accomplished for my world, my country, my family and, most especially, the world's children by the time I am ready to meet Saint Germain at the gates of heaven at the conclusion of this life?"

I myself pray fervently that you will have laid foundations sure and strong so that when the members of the seventh root race are ready to press their precious feet into the warm soil of Mother Earth for the very first time, you will have prepared a place for them not unlike the realms from which they have come....

I, Saint Germain, have sponsored you to have unlimited access to the violet flame as long as you do not misuse it. I am also sponsoring you to help me care for the children of South America and the world—children of the new age and children of earlier root races who should have long ago attained union with God but did not because their mentors did not teach them the path of ultimate self-realization.   (March 16, 1996)

The souls of the seventh root race will not grace your towns and cities unless you prove to your spiritual hierarchs that you will care for the children who are already in your midst. Since souls of light have volunteered to embody among the poorest of the poor and since those of high attainment also move among them, you must assume—and you dare not deny it—that God has placed his divine spark within each and every one of them.

Now, if you are convinced that this is so, then you must act upon your conviction. For to turn your back on the homeless children is tantamount to turning your back on your own "inner child" or your "inner children," as some psychologists have called the components of the soul....

You simply cannot turn your backs on these souls, for they, together with your own children, have the potential to bring in the golden age—if you will only teach them. Yes, teach the children!

(March 4, 1996)

These souls of the seventh root race are not simply the holy innocents. They have been preparing. ...They have tremendous talent....Let them be born as warriors of peace.   (April 7, 1996)

I want to see that prophesied golden age. I want to see the coming of the seventh root race!

(July 4, 1996)

A Key to Turning Back Prophecy

Turning around this one thing, beloved, can be a staying action on all other predictions that I have given you concerning nuclear war and earth changes. The stopping of the slaying of the innocents—this is the key to the reprieve and the key to the mercy out of the heart of Mother Mary as she does intercede for the nations before the throne of grace. (July 4, 1991)

Saint Germain is referring here to the millions of souls denied incarnation since the 1973 Supreme Court decision of *Roe v. Wade*. I know that abortion is a very controversial issue but in the true spirit of prophecy, I am obliged to share what may be a new perspective for you on this subject.

Two students of mine, a man and wife who are health-care professionals, once told me how troubled they were to see children being born into "underprivileged" families. On the other hand, they were also concerned about the physical and emotional traumas that sometimes plague women who have had an abortion. But from their perspective, abortion was a better alternative than being born into a poor or negligent family.

I listened quietly and when they were finished talking I simply said, "All that may be true. But you're not looking at it from the child's perspective."

They were silent and stunned. The child's perspective? They hadn't thought about it in that way before.

The Child's Perspective

What is the perspective of the unborn child? From the soul's point of view, the most painful and tragic consequence of abortion is that it aborts the divine plan of their soul—the special mission in life they have been waiting to fulfill, sometimes for thousands of years. Abortion also cuts short the divine plan of entire groups of souls who are tied together by their karma and cannot complete their mission because part of their "team" didn't make it into embodiment.

All of us have a date with our destiny and with our karma. If we miss the date, then we miss our opportunity to pay off old debts that we owe certain individuals. And if we miss our cycle of opportunity, we may not get it again for a long, long time. Very often the child has karma with the parents and vice versa. Aborting the child may prevent them all from balancing their karma with each other and from fulfilling their spiritual mission for that embodiment.

What's just as troublesome is that souls who need to reincarnate so that they can balance their karma are finding it more and more difficult to do so. There have been between 1 billion and 1.5 billion abortions worldwide since 1973. In the United States alone, at least 36 million abortions have been performed since the *Roe v. Wade* decision—an equivalent of 7.5 percent of the current U.S. population.

These "missing persons" will not take their place as adults on the world scene in the twenty-first century, nor will those who might have been their offspring. The absence of these souls in embodiment in this hour has compromised the divine plan for earth, and the karma created by it cannot even be calculated. We are the losers and this karma affects us all. It is a karma upon our entire civilization.

Once these two health-care professionals started thinking about the issue from the child's point of view, they totally changed their own perspective on the situation. They made a decision to make amends for the karma they had created by promoting abortion both in their personal and professional lives.

Together they went on to have two more children of their own, even though they were both in their forties. In addition, the husband went on to write a book about the spiritual and psychological consequences of abortion on the mother. Several years later a young woman came by to thank him for writing his book. She pointed to her three-year-old son and said, "My little one wouldn't be here today if you hadn't written that book."

An Upset in the Spiritual Ecosystem

Mother Mary has described the frustration of souls who are not able to meet their timetables:

There are souls who have been denied life who have a tremendous anguish and frustration that they are not in embodiment to help you meet the crisis of your cities and your nations, every crisis that besets you this day. One of the principal reasons why there is such crisis is that those whom God has sent to be here when these challenges were to come upon earth are not in embodiment....

Such an upset of the spiritual-cosmic ecosystem has not been so rampant upon earth since the last days of Atlantis.   (Oct. 26, 1990)

The Laws of Universal Life

Saint Germain holds the rights of each individual as paramount. But individuality, he says, exists in consideration of the rights of others and the rights of the community. Individuality does not confer the right to take life. And nature has always exacted a recompense for man's inhumanity to man. Family planning and the use of safe contraceptives are important, but birth control starts before conception. (Abortion is acceptable when there is jeopardy to the life of the mother.)

Saint Germain has said that "a nation is vulnerable who has not defended life in the womb.... Life must become sensitive to life." That was Saint Germain's message as he gave the following prophecy through me on a television show in 1982, where I said:

Human government founded since Noah has been founded to protect human life. The nation or the government that creates legislation allowing murder is doomed to go down. It will go down by cataclysm. It will go down by economic collapse. But it will go down because it is not consistent with the laws of universal life.... Abortion is first-degree murder of God....

That is a fiat of Almighty God. I didn't originate it, but it has the power of the Holy Spirit. It will come to pass. And if America does not refute legislated, legalized, tax-supported murder, the judgment will come as it came upon Judah and every other nation who has practiced it.[2]

Dr. Helen Wambach's Research

The solution to the karmic dilemma of abortion is *not* threatening or killing abortion providers or making threats against abortion clinics. The solution is compassionately providing a safe haven for the parents and their children.

We, individually and as communities, can support single mothers and mothers-to-be. We can also pray for mothers to carry their babies to term and, if they do not wish to raise them, to put them up for adoption. There are thousands of couples eagerly awaiting the opportunity to adopt a child.

The fascinating work of Dr. Helen Wambach gives us a glimpse into the spiritual life of the unborn child and the issue of adoption. Dr. Wambach was a clinical psychologist and regression-therapy expert who pioneered past-life and pre-natal research. One of the most interesting conclusions of Dr. Wambach's research is that some of her subjects who were adopted children said while under hypnosis that they knew *before* they were born that they were destined to be adopted. It was part of their life plan.

"Some of them knew before they were born of the relationship they would have with the adoptive parents," says Dr. Wambach, "and felt that they would not be able to come to them as their own genetic child but chose the method of adoption as a way to reach their parents." Her research led her to conclude that "chance and accident apparently played no part in the adoption."[3]

This puts a new light on the attitude among some people today that "if you are pregnant and don't want to keep your child, you might as well abort it." In fact, it may be someone's karma and destiny to give birth to a certain child and then put him up for adoption so that the child can find his rightful parents, who are unable to have children.

Saint Germain encourages those who are able to

have children to provide a home for souls waiting to take their place on the stage of life. He says:

> Let many parents rise up out of the new age movement, those who are the spiritual ones, and offer to give birth to not one but several children, that they might bring in those who have been denied.
>
> (April 27, 1991)

We can also pray that souls who have been aborted and are waiting to incarnate will find parents to sponsor them and love them.

Those who have supported abortion and want to balance that karma should realize that God is merciful and has given us a way to become sponsors of life. We can rectify our karma not only through prayer work but also by giving birth to children or by adopting or sponsoring children financially. We can participate in community programs, become a mentor, or support organizations that care for underprivileged children or Tibetan children, for example.

George Washington's Vision of Three Perils

During the harsh winter of 1777 in Valley Forge, Pennsylvania, a turning point for the Revolutionary War, George Washington saw a vision of three perils that would face America. They are sobering. The first two visions have already come to pass as the Revolutionary War and the Civil War.

The third prophecy, Washington said, was the "most fearful." Referring to George Washington's vision, Saint Germain said:

> If [Washington's] third vision comes to pass because men have not heeded my call, ... and because those in office, though they have known my name, have not called to me for aid—if there should be war upon this soil, it will be turned back only by divine intervention. This is the prophecy, beloved ones.
>
> (Nov. 27, 1986)

The following account was originally published by Wesley Bradshaw and was reprinted in the National Tribune in December 1880.

George Washington's Vision

The last time I ever saw Anthony Sherman was on the fourth of July, 1859, in Independence Square. He was then ninety-nine years old, and becoming very feeble. But though so old, his dimming eyes rekindled as he gazed upon Independence Hall, which he came to visit once more.

"Let us go into the hall," he said. "I want to tell you of an incident of Washington's life—one which no one alive knows of except myself; and, if you live you will before long, see it verified.

"From the opening of the Revolution we experienced all phases of fortune, now good and now ill, one time victorious and another conquered. The darkest period we had, I think, was when Washington after several reverses, retreated to Valley Forge, where he resolved to pass the winter of 1777.

"Ah! I have often seen the tears coursing down our dear commander's care-worn cheeks, as he would be conversing with a confidential officer about the condition of his poor soldiers. You have doubtless heard the story of Washington's going into the thicket to pray. Well, it was not only true, but he used often to pray in secret for aid and comfort from God, the interposition of whose Divine Providence brought us safely through the darkest days of tribulation.

"One day, I remember it well, the chilly winds whistled through the leafless trees, though the sky was cloudless and the sun shone brightly, he remained in his quarters nearly all the afternoon alone. When he came out I noticed that his face was a shade paler than usual, and there seemed to be something on his mind of more than ordinary importance.

"Returning just after dusk, he dispatched an orderly to the quarters of the officer I mention who was presently in attendance. After a preliminary conversation of about half an hour, Washington, gazing upon his companion with that strange look of dignity which he alone could command, said to the latter:

"'I do not know whether it is owing to the anxiety of my mind, or what, but this afternoon as I was sitting at this table engaged in preparing a dispatch, something seemed to disturb me. Looking up, I beheld standing opposite me a singularly beautiful female. So astonished was I, for I had given strict orders not to be disturbed that it was some moments before I found language to inquire into the cause of her presence.

"'A second, a third, and even a fourth time did I repeat my question, but received no answer from my mysterious visitor except a slight raising of her eyes. By this time I felt strange sensations spreading through me. I would have risen but the riveted gaze of the being before me rendered volition impossible. I assayed once more to address her, but my tongue had become useless. Even thought itself had become paralyzed. A new influence, mysterious, potent, irresistible, took possession of me. All I could do was to gaze steadily, vacantly at my unknown visitant.

"Look and Learn"

"'Gradually the surrounding atmosphere seemed as though becoming filled with sensations, and luminous. Everything about me seemed to rarify—the mysterious visitor herself becoming more airy and yet more distinct to my sight than before.

I now began to feel as one dying, or rather to experience the sensations which I have sometimes imagined accompany dissolution. I did not think, I did not reason, I did not move; all were alike impossible. I was only conscious of gazing fixedly, vacantly at my companion.

"'Presently I heard a voice saying, "Son of the Republic, look and learn," while at the same time my visitor extended her arm eastwardly. I now beheld a heavy white vapor at some distance rising fold upon fold. This gradually dissipated, and I looked upon a strange scene. Before me lay spread out in one vast plain all the countries of the world—Europe, Asia, Africa and America. I saw rolling and tossing between Europe and America the billows of the Atlantic, and between Asia and America lay the Pacific.

"'"Son of the Republic," said the same mysterious voice as before, "look and learn." At that moment I beheld a dark, shadowy being, like an angel, standing, or rather floating in mid-air, between Europe and America. Dipping water out of the ocean in the hollow of each hand, he sprinkled some upon America with his right hand, while with his left hand he cast some on Europe.

"'Immediately a cloud raised from these countries, and joined in mid-ocean. For a while it remained stationary, and then moved slowly westward, until it enveloped America in its murky folds. Sharp flashes of lightning gleamed through it at intervals, and I heard the smothered groans and cries of the American people. A second time the angel dipped water from the ocean, and sprinkled it out as before. The dark cloud was then drawn back to the ocean, in whose heaving billows it sank from view.

"'A third time I heard the mysterious voice saying, "Son of the Republic, look and learn." I cast my eyes upon America and beheld villages and towns and cities springing up one after another until the whole land from the Atlantic to the Pacific was dotted with them. Again, I heard the mysterious voice say, "Son of the Republic, the end of the century cometh, look and learn."

"'At this the dark shadowy angel turned his face southward, and from Africa I saw an ill-omened spectre approach our land. It flitted slowly over every town and city of the latter. The inhabitants presently set themselves in battle array against each other.

"'As I continued looking I saw a bright angel, on whose brow rested a crown of light, on which was traced the word "Union," bearing the American flag which he placed between the divided nation, and said, *Remember ye are brethren.*"

"'Instantly, the inhabitants, casting from them their weapons became friends once more, and united around the National Standard.

Divine Intervention

"'And again I heard the mysterious voice saying, "Son of the Republic, look and learn." At this the dark, shadowy angel placed a trumpet to his mouth, and blew three distinct blasts; and taking water from the ocean, he sprinkled it upon Europe, Asia and Africa.

"'Then my eyes beheld a fearful scene: from each of these countries arose thick, black clouds that were soon joined into one. And throughout this mass there gleamed a dark red light by which I saw hordes of armed men, who, moving with the cloud, marched by land and sailed by sea to America, which country was enveloped in the volume of cloud.

"'And I dimly saw these vast armies devastate the whole country and burn the villages, towns and cities that I beheld springing up. As my ears listened to the thundering of the cannon, clashing of swords, and the shouts and cries of millions in mortal combat, I heard again the mysterious voice saying, "Son of the Republic, look and learn." When the voice had ceased, the dark shadowy angel placed his trumpet once more to his mouth, and blew a long and fearful blast.

"'Instantly a light as of a thousand suns shone down from above me, and pierced and broke into fragments the dark cloud which enveloped America. At the same moment the angel upon whose head still shone the word Union, and who bore our national flag in one hand and a sword in the other, descended from the heavens attended by legions of white spirits. These joined the inhabitants of America, who I perceived were well-nigh overcome, but who immediately taking courage again, closed up their broken ranks and renewed the battle.

"'Again, amid the fearful noise of the conflict, I heard the mysterious voice saying, "Son of the Republic, look and learn." As the voice ceased, the shadowy angel for the last time dipped water from the ocean and sprinkled it upon America. Instantly the dark cloud rolled back, together with the armies it had brought, leaving the inhabitants of the land victorious.

"'Then once more I beheld the villages, towns and cities springing up where I had seen them before, while the bright angel, planting the azure standard he had brought in the midst of them, cried with a loud voice: *While the stars remain, and the heavens send down dew upon the earth, so long shall the Union last."* And taking from his brow the crown on which blazoned the word "Union," he placed it upon the Standard while the people, kneeling down, said, "Amen."

"'The scene instantly began to fade and dissolve, and I at last saw nothing but the rising, curling vapor I at first beheld. This also disappearing, I found myself once more gazing upon the mysterious visitor, who, in the same voice I had heard before, said, "Son of the Republic, what you have seen is thus interpreted:

"'"Three great perils will come upon the Republic. The most fearful is the third passing which the whole world united shall not prevail against her. Let every child of the Republic learn to live for his God, his land and Union."

"'With these words the vision vanished, and I started from my seat and felt that I had seen a vision wherein had been shown to me the birth, progress, and destiny of the United States.'

"Such, my friends," concluded the venerable narrator, "were the words I heard from Washington's own lips, and America will do well to profit by them."

A Bold Vision of Aquarius

Those who understand the real purpose of prophecy know that the events of the next two thousand years are not predestined. As Saint Germain tells us, prophecy offers enlightened men and women the opportunity to unite and determine that the negatives will not come to pass.

Aquarius is the entrance into a vast cosmos.... Beloved ones, come what may, be pioneers of the Spirit....

Determine to pass through the eye of the needle...and to hold before you the vision of that light at the end of the tunnel....

My vision of the age of Aquarius is one of endurance—those enduring the soul-testing and the path of initiation, receiving the crown of life....

My vision of this age is that you will lay a foundation when it is possible to lay that foundation and that you, by the gathering of your knowledge and your professional experience from all walks of life, will be ready to lay that upon the altar of God and see how the new age may start and have a new chance, no longer infiltrated in every field by the betrayers of the people.

I envision an age when life in its wholeness can truly be lived, for the practitioners in health may deliver what God designed to be the answer to all physical burdens and problems....

[Aquarius] is indeed a new cosmic cycle and a new beginning. And this is why we desire to see you be there to enjoy the fruits of your labors and the momentum of your victory, to be there and to launch a new era....

My vision is for the victory, beloved. And my vision for you is that you will find in the ingenuity of your souls the means to...raise up the green shoot of new life on earth. Let the green shoot be the sign of Aquarius....

You will not know until all is said and done on planet earth just how much you have counted for the light and for the victory. I send you forth, for you alone can pass your tests. You alone must figure out and calculate how you will achieve your victory, given the equation of an age.

(May 21, 1989)

PART II

Spiritual Solutions

The only way to predict the future is to have power to shape the future.

—ERIC HOFFER

13 A High-Frequency Spiritual Energy

*Destiny is not a matter of chance,
it is a matter of choice.*
—WILLIAM JENNINGS BRYAN

Masters of the Oriental art of Feng Shui know all about energy flow. They teach that clutter and the arrangement of our physical environment determine the flow of energy *(chi)* in our surroundings. That flow of energy, or lack of it, they say, powerfully affects our health, our finances, our relationships—the very course of our life.

In exactly the same way, the flow of energy at subtle levels *within* our being affects the circumstances of our life. It affects our physical and emotional well-being. It affects our spiritual progress. It even affects the kinds of events and people that move in and out of our life. When energy is flowing freely, we feel peaceful, healthy, creative and happy. When it is blocked, we can experience everything from frustration, sluggishness and depression to accidents and disease.

A major factor in energy flow is karma. Karma is the effect of causes we have set in motion in the past, whether ten minutes ago or ten embodiments ago. We have all grown up learning about karma. We just didn't call it that. Instead, we heard: *What goes around comes around. Whatsoever a man soweth, that shall he also reap. For every action there is an equal and opposite reaction. And in the end, the love you take is equal to the love you make…*

Karmic Clutter

Just as clutter in our environment can cause stagnation in our life, so karmic clutter in our mind, body and emotions can cause stagnation. And we all have some karmic clutter. For while we have done much good in our lifetimes, at one time or another we have done things we are not happy about.

Every moment energy is flowing to us from God, and every moment we are deciding whether we will put a positive or negative spin on it. By the law of the circle, the law of karma, that energy will return to us. When the positive energy returns, we see positive things come into our life. The energy that has our negative stamp on it, because we have used that energy to harm rather than help others, also returns to its source—this time seeking resolution. It returns to us as opportunity to make things right.

When we don't transform that returning energy into something positive, it doesn't just go away. It collects and then calcifies in our physical, mental or emotional worlds. As a result of this karmic clutter, we don't feel as light, free, happy, vibrant and spiritual as we could.

Negative energy can also build up on a large scale when groups of people contribute, for instance, to pollution, prejudice, persecution. When this "group karma" returns en masse, it can have large-scale consequences, such as the wars or earth changes that prophets have foreseen for our time. How we deal with our individual and group karma will determine whether these prophecies will come to pass.

Rising to New Levels of Realization

Karma is the great x factor in our spiritual progress. As our sponsor for the Aquarian age, Saint Germain wants to help us solve our karmic dilemmas so we can realize our highest potential. His solution: the violet flame, an accelerated, high-frequency spiritual energy that transmutes (transforms) negative karma into positive energy. He says:

> Karma is the weight that prevents the soul from flying. Karma affects all choices. It affects contracts —business, marriage and otherwise—those who are drawn to your life and those who cannot be, the children you may give birth to.
>
> Every day as percentages of karma pass through the violet flame and you ratify that transmutation by good deeds, words and works of love and service, you are lightening the load and therefore rising to new planes of realization, new associations.... The less karma you have, the greater your opportunity day by day.   (April 16, 1988)

Those of us who have regularly used the violet flame in our prayers have watched it ease the burden and suffering of family and friends. It has enhanced our creativity and helped us overcome blocks to healing physical problems or emotional hang-ups. It has helped us navigate through major life challenges. It has helped us forgive others and move beyond painful experiences.

With regular use, the violet flame can bring positive change into your life—and transmute the build-up of mankind's karma that could result in the darkness prophesied for our time. That is why Saint Germain says that prophecy is not set in stone.

The True Meaning of Prophecy

Prophecy is a warning of what will happen if nothing changes. It is not predestination. Prophecies can be mitigated or turned back if mankind change their ways, pray for divine intercession and transmute their karma with the violet flame before that karma crystallizes and becomes physical.

In short, the violet flame affords us the optimum opportunity for self-transformation and world transformation. That is exactly why Saint Germain, out of his great compassion for our souls, gave us the gift of the violet flame in this century.

The violet flame has long been used by spiritual adepts. In the past it was also used by the people of Atlantis when their golden-age civilization was at its height. Because they eventually misused the violet flame, in later centuries only the few were entrusted with its secrets. But in the early 1930s, Saint Germain founded the I AM movement and reintroduced the violet flame to the world.

Transmuting Personal Karma ahead of Time

Today Saint Germain is sponsoring us to use the violet flame because he wants us to overcome the karmic challenges that loom on the horizon before they have a chance to weigh us down. For he knows that unless we invoke the violet flame to transmute our negative karma, sooner or later we will be compelled to balance it in other ways—ways that may severely restrict our options.

We may have to enter into painful life experiences with those we have wronged or those we have had bad relationships with in the past. Or we may have to bear our karma in our bodies as discomfort, disease, accident or sometimes even premature death. Saint Germain says:

> What, then, of physical karma? Does it portend the expected events?...
>
> Karma shall be mitigated for those who one by one have kept the flame, who shall keep the flame, who will be in the center of the roaring violet flame....
>
> Thus that which you transmute ahead of time is not there to descend in your individual world.
>
> (April 15, 1990)

The Spiritual Flames

Just as a ray of sunlight passing through a prism is refracted into the seven colors of the rainbow, so spiritual light manifests as seven rays, or flames. When we call forth the spiritual flames in our prayers and meditations, each flame creates a specific action in our body, mind and soul. The violet flame is the color and frequency of spiritual light that stimulates mercy, justice, freedom and transmutation.

To "transmute" is to alter in form, appearance or nature, especially to change something into a higher form. The term was used by alchemists who attempted to transmute base metals into gold, separating the "subtle" from the "gross" by means of heat. The real purpose of alchemical transmutation was spiritual transformation and the attainment of eternal life. That is precisely what the violet flame can do for us. It separates out the "gross" elements of our karma from the gold of our true inner self so that we can achieve lasting spiritual transformation.

Why is the violet flame so powerful? In our physical world, violet light has the shortest wavelength, and therefore the highest frequency, in the visible spectrum. Since frequency is directly proportional to energy, the violet light also has the most energy. That means that it also has the greatest ability to change matter at the atomic level.

Edgar Cayce recognized the healing power of the violet ray. In over nine hundred of his readings, he recommended an electrical device—a "violet ray" machine that emits a violet-colored electrical charge—to treat several ailments, including exhaustion, lethargy, poor circulation, digestive problems and nervous disorders.

How Does the Violet Flame Work?

Saint Germain explains that the violet flame has the ability to change physical conditions because, of all the flames, the violet is closest in vibratory action to the components of matter. "The violet flame can combine with any molecule or molecular structure, any particle of matter known or unknown, and any wave of light, electron or electricity," he says. Wherever people gather together to give violet-flame prayers, "there you notice immediately an improvement in physical conditions."

The violet flame can literally consume the debris within and between the atoms of your being. It's like soaking them in a chemical solution that, layer by layer, dissolves the dirt that has been trapped there for thousands of years.

When you call forth the violet flame, it sets up a polarity between the nucleus of the atom and the white-fire core of the flame. The nucleus, being matter, assumes the negative pole; the white-fire core of the violet flame, being Spirit, assumes the positive pole.

The interaction between the nucleus of the atom and the light in the violet flame establishes an oscillation. This oscillation dislodges the densities that are trapped between the electrons orbiting the nucleus. As this hardened substance that weighs down the atom is loosened, it is thrown into the violet flame. On contact with the violet flame, the dense substance is cleansed, purified and restored to its native purity. Freed of this debris, the electrons begin to move more freely, thus raising our spiritual vibration and our energy levels. This action takes place at nonphysical, or "metaphysical," dimensions of matter.

The Ultimate Time-Management Tool

The violet flame is the oil in the gears of life. It's what can make things go more smoothly and more quickly. In fact, Saint Germain says it's the ultimate time-management tool:

> I know that the desire is upon your heart to know and understand what God has appointed you to do in this life and in previous lifetimes. I know that you have a deep desiring to fulfill all things so that you might arrive at the gate of the next world having fully accomplished your mission.
>
> I can assure you that the violet flame will assist you in accelerating both that mission and those spirals of light that are in every atom and cell of your being. I assure you that you can encapsulate time and accelerate time and that you will find yourself accomplishing in ten years what without the violet flame could take you a century.
>
> The violet flame does shorten the distance. It

does increase the capacity of every moment and hour. It accelerates the functioning of the mind and the ability of the body to be rejuvenated....

If you look for the revitalizing,...call forth showers upon showers upon showers of living violet flame.   (Oct. 14, 1991)

The violet flame can indeed facilitate our healing, but it is an adjunct to sound medical measures, not a substitute for them. The violet flame will work for us, but we have to work with it. We need to be sensible about following the basic laws of health, diet and wholesome living, and consult our doctor. Medical science has much to offer and if surgery is necessary, then we should avail ourselves of it.

Violet Flame in a Near-Death Experience

Dannion Brinkley in his book *Saved by the Light* gives an eye-opening account of his near-death experiences. Like others who have had near-death experiences, he tells of going through a tunnel and being escorted by a being of light. But unlike other NDEers, he remembers where he went and what he saw with much more detail.

During his first NDE, a being of light led Dannion to a city of crystal cathedrals, which were really halls of learning. At one of these cathedrals, thirteen beings of light revealed to him events that would take place in the future. Of the 117 revelations he recalls, almost 100 have come to pass. Dannion says that many of the prophecies I've included in this book are directly connected to what his spiritual advisors showed him.

Dannion spoke about his life-changing experiences at a spiritual conference we held in July 1997. After that, he told me that during his near-death sojourns he saw the violet flame. "I have seen the violet flame and felt the violet flame," he said. "When you pass from this world to the next, you automatically become the flame. You connect to it. I have done it. When you pass through the violet flame, you are connected to a new dimension."

"Every crystal city," he added, "has the violet flame as well as all the spiritual flames. But the violet flame is the greatest of the flames. The violet flame is the purest place of love. It's what really empowers you."

Dannion went on to share with me what he has learned about the violet flame. "The violet flame is a light that serves all spiritual heritages, that gives respect and dignity to all things. It gives us a way to connect with each other. That flame is inside of us. The flame *is* us.

"A new world is coming. It will change every day. Yes, there will be some turbulent moments, but it's changing for the better. And the violet flame will come and it will grow, and you who work with that flame will be contributors to that new world. If you have one thing that grows and glows brighter than anything else in the innermost part of your being— the violet flame—then no matter what transitions we go through in the coming years, you will have a quiet, peaceful place within."

Working with the Flame

In September 1997, Dannion was back in the hospital and very near death—again. During that difficult period, I called him every day and prayed for him. Members of our community worldwide prayed for him as well. After his recovery, he told a group of my students, "Many of you prayed for me with the violet flame and sent me your love as I was struggling between life and death. I could feel that love, I could see the violet flame, I could hear it. Those prayers brought me back—that's the power of the flame.

"The greatness of the violet flame is that it doesn't produce heat; it produces love. Now, sometimes love gets a little heated, but love in itself is pure power. And that's pleasant, that's cozy. It's like an early spring morning or an early fall, somewhere in between.

"In order to receive love in a higher, more powerful flame, you must give it. In your meditations, listen to the music of the flame and let it resonate through your souls. Then send that flame to others. Let it surround them. Let them feel that gentleness of the violet flame—that calm, peaceful place that we have served and loved. Let the flame touch them so that they can feel what it's like to touch their own reality—the flame that's within them."

We can get in touch with the gentle power of the violet flame through our prayers, meditations and decrees. Decrees are an accelerated prayer form, spoken aloud, that combines affirmations, prayers, meditations and visualizations.

The greatest revolutionaries, the revolutionaries of the spirit, saw prayer as one of the chief instruments of change. How many times have we turned on the TV set and looked on in dismay at the helpless children caught in the latest episode of ethnic cleansing? Or watched the victims of an earthquake or tornado digging through the rubble that used to be their home? How many times have we wondered how we could help? The creative power of sound gives us a way to do just that.

The Creative Power of Sound

Recent scientific advances and studies point to what sages knew thousands of years ago: sound holds the key to the mysteries of the universe.

We know that sound can destroy—a high-pitched note can shatter a wineglass, a sonic boom can crack plaster, a gunshot can set off an avalanche. But sound is also a constructive force, as doctors and health practitioners are discovering every day. Ultrasound (high-pitched sound waves) is being used for everything from cleaning wounds to diagnosing tumors to pulverizing kidney stones. Someday it may even be used to inject drugs into the body, making needles obsolete.

Scientists are now researching sound's impact on the brain. Certain kinds of classical music, by composers like Bach, Mozart and Beethoven, have a range of positive effects, including temporarily raising the IQ, expanding memory and speeding learning. Some alternative health practitioners are experimenting with using specific tones to heal the organs.

The creative power of sound is also at the heart of the world's spiritual traditions East and West. Hindu writings tell us that yogis have used mantras, along with visualizations, to light fires, materialize physical objects (such as food), bring rain and even influence the outcome of battles. Producing physical changes wasn't their primary goal, however. They believed that mantras brought them protection and wisdom, enhanced their concentration and meditation, and helped them achieve enlightenment and oneness with God.

The Jewish mystical tradition also speaks of the power of the spoken word. Kabbalists believe that by calling upon and meditating on the names of God, we tap into an infinite source of power that restores peace and harmony to this world. They say that Moses, for instance, had the ability to "shake the world" because he called on the name of the Lord. Catholic tradition tells us that Saint Clare of Assisi saved her convent during an attack by Saracens when she held up the Eucharist and prayed aloud.

An Interactive Relationship with Spirit

Like prayers, decrees are spoken petitions to God. But more than that, they are a command for the will of God to be manifest. When you use decrees, you are in effect commanding the flow of energy from Spirit to matter. You are entering into a partnership and an interactive relationship with God.

When we meditate, we commune with God. When we pray, we communicate with God and request his help. When we decree, we are communing, communicating and commanding. We are commanding God's light to enter our world for alchemical change. We are directing God to send his light and his angels into action for personal and world transformation.

Prayer, meditation and decrees are all ways of accessing the power of Spirit, and there is a time and place to practice each type of devotion. But decrees are the most powerful form of invoking God's light. Devotees of many different spiritual traditions have found that decrees enhance their own spiritual practice.

People often wonder: Is it really necessary to *ask* God to help us? Isn't he omniscient and doesn't he already know how to take care of our problems and our needs? Isaiah tells us, "Thus saith the Lord, the Holy One of Israel, and his Maker, 'Ask me of things to come concerning my sons, and concerning the work of my hands *command ye me.*'"[1] And the Lord said to Job, "Thou shalt make thy prayer unto him [the Almighty], and he shall hear thee.... Thou shalt also *decree a thing,* and it shall be established unto thee."[2]

It all comes down to the law of free will. God gave us free will because he wanted us to exercise our individuality. God doesn't go back on his word. He respects our free will. You can think of earth as a laboratory where God has given us the freedom to experiment and evolve. If, like an indulgent and overbearing parent, God rushed in to stop us every time we were about to make a mistake, we wouldn't experience the results of our actions—good and bad—and we wouldn't be able to learn our lessons for ourselves and thereby grow spiritually.

Send the Angels into Action

So according to God's laws, he and his angels may not intervene in human affairs unless we call to them for help. Sometimes all it takes is a quick prayer like *"Enter my life, O God! I can't do this without you! Send your angels to take command of this situation right now!"*—and then name the specific problem burdening you or a loved one.

Simple, quick prayers like this will bring the angels right into your home. Don't be meek when you make these calls. Give them as dynamic commands. The greater the fervor and intensity of your heart, the greater the response from heaven.

Saint Germain is deeply concerned about the conditions in our society that severely limit souls from reaching their highest potential, from poverty and child abuse to poor education and the plight of the homeless. He says that each one of us can make a supreme difference when we engage our free will in prayer.

He tells us that the angels are just waiting for us to call them into action to tackle these problems.[3]

He encourages us to frequently send them on assignments by giving quick, dynamic prayers and decrees throughout the day. He says we can even make lists of the conditions that need their attention and direct them to take command of those exact conditions in our prayers:

> I beg of you, if you shall remember one thing..., remember not to forget to assign the angels—not to forget to send them, to love them, to command them, to illumine them and be illumined by them.
>
> (Oct. 12, 1992)

The "I AM" as Empowerment

Decrees are based on a system of positive affirmations that use the name of God "I AM," or "I AM THAT I AM," to access spiritual power. When God revealed his name I AM THAT I AM to Moses, he said, "This is my name forever, and this is my memorial unto all generations." The Jerusalem Bible translates this passage as "This is my name for all time; by this name I shall be invoked for all generations to come." Here God is directing us to use his name to invoke his intercession.

I AM is more than a sacred name. It is an empowerment. It is a scientific formula. When you recite God's name with faith and love, God releases his energy as a stupendous waterfall of light to heal mind and body, heart and soul.

What does "I AM THAT I AM" mean? To me it means simply but profoundly "as above, so below." God is affirming, "I am here below that which I AM above." When you say, "I AM THAT I AM," you are affirming that God is where you are. In effect, you are saying: "As God is in heaven, so God is on earth within me. Right where I stand, God is. I am that 'I AM.'"

Jesus himself used the power of God's name "I AM" when he made statements like "I AM [i.e., God in me is] the resurrection and the life," "I AM the light of the world," "I AM come that they might have life and that they might have it more abundantly," and "I AM the way, the truth and the life."

You too can use the name of God "I AM" to create short, powerful affirmations. They are powerful because every time you say, "I AM...," you are really saying, "God in me is...." And whatever you affirm following the words "I AM" will become a reality in your world. This is why Saint Germain has given us his mantra for the Aquarian age: *I AM a being of violet fire! I AM the purity God desires!*, which means "God in me is a being of violet fire! God in me is the purity God desires!" When you make an affirmation like this, the light of God flowing through you will obey that command.[4]

The Chart of Your Divine Self

The reason we can call to God and he will answer is because we are connected to him. We are his sons and daughters. We have a direct relationship to God and he has placed a portion of himself in us. In order to better understand this relationship, the ascended masters have designed the Chart of Your Divine Self.

The Chart of Your Divine Self is a portrait of you and of the God within you. It is a diagram of yourself and your potential to become who you really are. It is an outline of your spiritual anatomy.

The upper figure is your "I AM Presence," the Presence of God that is individualized in each one of us. It is your personalized "I AM THAT I AM." Your I AM Presence is surrounded by seven concentric spheres of spiritual energy that make up what is called your "causal body." The spheres of pulsating energy contain the record of the good works you have performed since your very first incarnation on earth. They are like your cosmic bank account.

The Higher Self

The middle figure in the chart represents the "Holy Christ Self," who is also called the Higher Self. You can think of your Holy Christ Self as your chief guardian angel and dearest friend, your inner

The Chart of Your Divine Self

teacher and voice of conscience.

Just as the I AM Presence is the presence of God that is individualized for each of us, so the Holy Christ Self is the presence of the universal Christ that is individualized for each of us. "The Christ" is actually a title given to those who have attained oneness with their Higher Self, or Christ Self. That's why Jesus was called "Jesus, the Christ." *Christ* comes from the Greek word *christos,* meaning "anointed" —anointed with the light of God.

What the Chart shows is that each of us has a Higher Self, or "inner Christ," and that each of us is destined to become one with that Higher Self— whether we call it the Christ, the Buddha, the Tao or the Atman. This "inner Christ" is what the Christian mystics sometimes refer to as the "inner man of the heart," and what the Upanishads mysteriously describe as a being the "size of a thumb" who "dwells deep within the heart."

We all have moments when we feel that connection with our Higher Self—when we are creative, loving, joyful. But there are other moments when we feel out of sync with our Higher Self—moments when we become angry, depressed, lost. What the spiritual path is all about is learning to sustain the connection to the higher part of ourselves so that we can make our greatest contribution to humanity.

The Divine Spark

The shaft of white light descending from the I AM Presence through the Holy Christ Self to the lower figure in the Chart is the crystal cord (sometimes called the silver cord). It is the "umbilical cord," the lifeline, that ties you to Spirit.

Your crystal cord also nourishes that special, radiant flame of God that is ensconced in the secret chamber of your heart. It is called the threefold flame, or divine spark, because it is literally a spark of sacred fire that God has transmitted from his heart to yours. This flame is called "threefold" because it engenders the primary attributes of Spirit —power, wisdom and love.

The mystics of the world's religions have contacted the divine spark, describing it as the seed of divinity within. Buddhists, for instance, speak of the "germ of Buddhahood" that exists in every living being. In the Hindu tradition, the Katha Upanishad speaks of the "light of the Spirit" that is concealed in the "secret high place of the heart" of all beings.

Likewise, the fourteenth-century Christian theologian and mystic Meister Eckhart teaches of the divine spark when he says, "God's seed is within us." There is a part of us, says Eckhart, that "remains eternally in the Spirit and is divine.... Here God glows and flames without ceasing."

When we decree, we meditate on the flame in the secret chamber of our heart. This secret chamber is your own private meditation room, your interior castle, as Teresa of Avila called it. In Hindu tradition, the devotee visualizes a jeweled island in his heart. There he sees himself before a beautiful altar, where he worships his teacher in deep meditation.

Jesus spoke of entering the secret chamber of the heart when he said: "When thou prayest, enter into thy closet, and when thou hast shut thy door, pray to thy Father which is in secret; and thy Father which seeth in secret shall reward thee openly."

When I was a little girl I kept wondering: "What kind of closets did the disciples go into? Did people have closets in those days? You can't go into a closet—there's not enough air in there! What in the world is Jesus talking about?" Later on I realized that going into your closet to pray is going into another dimension of consciousness. It's entering into the heart and closing the door on the outside world.

Your Soul's Potential

The lower figure in the Chart of Your Divine Self represents you on the spiritual path, surrounded by the violet flame and the protective white light of God. The soul is the living potential of God—

the part of you that is mortal but that can become immortal.

The purpose of your soul's evolution on earth is to grow in self-mastery, balance your karma[5] and fulfill your mission on earth so that you can return to the spiritual dimensions that are your real home. When your soul at last takes flight and ascends back to God and the heaven-world, you will become an "ascended" master, free from the rounds of karma and rebirth.

The high-frequency energy of the violet flame can help you reach that goal more quickly.

14 The Mind-Body Connection

We are what we think,
having become what we thought.
—THE DHAMMAPADA

It's a spiritual axiom that whatever you put your mind on and whatever you pour your heart into will come true. That's why our thoughts and dreams, our hopes and visions are all-important. And that's why what you think about while you are praying or decreeing makes a big difference in how effective your prayers and decrees are. It's the mind-body connection.

If you are concentrating on your Higher Self or on the flame in your heart while you pray, you are energizing yourself with that light and taking on those spiritual patterns. If, on the other hand, you put your attention on negativity or lower vibrations, you will take on those patterns. That is why, for example, violence on TV or in movies is not a healthy diet for children or adults.

When we are dealing with prophecies, it's important to do the spiritual work to mitigate them, but *we must always keep our eye on the positive outcome.* We must visualize the highest good we can imagine—peace on earth, brotherhood, a clean environment. For what we together focus on, we will create.

Creative Visualizations

Our visualizations are a magnet that attracts the creative energies of Spirit to fill the blueprint we hold in mind. If many people concentrate on a negative outcome to a situation, they will consciously or unconsciously make it a reality. As Teilhard de Chardin said, "The whole of life lies in the verb *seeing*."

A good starting place for your visualizations is to focus on your I AM Presence, which you can see as a blazing sun of light overhead. You can also concentrate on the divine spark in your heart and see it as a dazzling sphere of light as brilliant as the sun at noonday. As you decree, see thousands of sunbeams going forth from your heart to heal and comfort those in need.

In your daily prayers, decrees and meditations,

try visualizing, as if on a movie screen, the desired outcome of your prayers. See taking place before your eyes the actions described in each word of the decree. Use your imagination to picture the resolution of the situations you are praying for.

If, for instance, you are decreeing to clean up pollution in the oceans, see in your mind's eye all marine life charged with the violet light and the oceans turning a beautiful violet hue. If you are decreeing to quell tensions in the Middle East, see the various factions throwing down their weapons and embracing each other as brothers and sisters. In the next chapter, we have included some suggested visualizations and meditations you can use while giving your prayers and decrees.

Be as specific as possible in your visualizations —and have fun with them. The more centered, concentrated and creative you are, the better your results will be.

Self-Fulfilling Prophecies

Our visualizations are self-fulfilling prophecies. But so are our words. In the last chapter we talked about the power of God's name "I AM" and said that whatever we affirm following the words "I AM" will become a reality in our world. This is because the light of God flowing through us will obey our command. That is yet another way of understanding the mind-body connection. The state of your body is influenced not only by what you think but by what you *say*. Spoken words command energy.

When you come to a place where you realize that the tremendous energy of God is flowing through you every moment, you have a sense of reverence and awe. You say to yourself, "Here is God's energy. What will I do with it today? Will I use God's energy to reinforce the negative side of life? Or will I use it to affirm something beautiful, something real, something that matters to my spiritual progress and that benefits others?"

Energizing the Body with Prayer

Another aspect of the mind-body connection and prayer has to do with building a momentum. People often ask, "Why should I have to ask God for something more than once?" Repeating a decree is not simply making a request over and over. It is an energy equation. Each time you repeat a decree, you are building a momentum. You are intensifying the power of the decree as you energize it with more and more of God's light.

In the East, people repeat their mantras over and over, even thousands of times a day, but in the West many of us are not accustomed to the idea of repeating a prayer. Yet both mystics and scientists have demonstrated the benefits of repetitive prayer.

The mystics of the Eastern Orthodox Church have a tradition of repeating the simple prayer "Lord Jesus Christ, Son of God, have mercy upon me" thousands of times. Over the centuries, monks who have done this have reported extraordinary mystical experiences and a feeling of oneness with God.

Medieval monks claimed that after several weeks of repeating this prayer for many hours, they entered an altered state. They said they could see a powerful light around them, which they compared to the light the disciples saw on Jesus' face and garments when he was transfigured.

A group of modern-day Benedictine monks discovered an unexpected benefit from their use of sound in giving Gregorian chants: their chanting seemed to energize their bodies. For hundreds of years the monks of the Benedictine order had kept a rigorous schedule, sleeping only a few hours a night and chanting from six to eight hours a day. When a new abbot changed the schedule and cut out the chanting, the monks became tired and lethargic. The more sleep they got, the more tired they seemed to become.

In 1967 Alfred Tomatis, a French physician, psychologist and ear specialist, was called in to find out what was wrong with them. He found that the monks had, in fact, been "chanting in order to 'charge' themselves."[1] He reintroduced chanting, along with a program of listening to stimulating sounds, and the monks soon found the energy to return to their normal schedule.

Dr. Herbert Benson, president and founder of the Mind/Body Medical Institute at Harvard Medical School, found that those who repeated Sanskrit mantras for as little as ten minutes a day experienced physiological changes—reduced heart rate, lower stress levels and slower metabolism. Repeating mantras also lowered the blood pressure of those who had high blood pressure and generally decreased the subjects' oxygen consumption, indicating that the body was in a restful state.

Subsequent studies documented in Benson's *Timeless Healing* found that repeating mantras can benefit the immune system, relieve insomnia, reduce visits to the doctor and even increase self-esteem. Benson and his colleagues also tested other prayers, including "Lord Jesus Christ, have mercy on me," and found that they had the same effect.

Positive Energy

At spiritual dimensions, here's why repeating our prayers and decrees is important: Every moment

God's energy is flowing to you from your I AM Presence through your crystal cord. So while you are giving your decrees, you are continuously charging the energy moving through you with God's power. The more you decree, the more positive energy you can send out into the world for the blessing of yourself and others.

Imagine you are sitting on the bank of a river and you pour a gallon of purple dye into it. The water in front of you turns a deep purple, but as soon as that section of the river moves downstream, the water in front of you is clear again. If you wanted to color the entire river purple, you would have to keep pouring huge vats of purple dye into it.

It's the same way with decreeing. Even if you decree for only a few minutes, your decrees will affect a situation. But sometimes a condition is so serious that it needs ongoing decree work. Saying a decree once is not enough to overcome major challenges.

For example, if you are considering a major career change and you want to be sure of your next step, you would probably want to decree daily for God's direction in your life until you feel sure that you have the answer. If you are concerned about a loved one who is undergoing surgery, you would give healing decrees on his or her behalf throughout the entire operation and the healing process.

If there is a crisis on the world scene, you would want to continue praying on that issue each day until you see a definite improvement in the situation. When we are dealing, as we are today, with a large accumulation of world karma that has been building up over centuries and centuries, then it will take a commensurate worldwide effort to transmute the karma before it becomes physical. Saint Germain has told us:

> I remind you that the days and the hours are moving swiftly. The cause of saving planet earth is not one that we can take down from the shelf today and put back on the shelf tomorrow.... Through your violet-flame decrees we can mitigate earth changes or eliminate them entirely.   (March 16, 1996)

> The violet flame is the mighty mitigating factor. ...Let all who know of the violet flame give it as a gift from my heart to every stranger they meet....
> Tell all the nations and tell all the people that the violet flame is their hope.   (July 4, 1987)

The Heart Connection

We've been talking about the mind-body connection, but the scientific power of prayer is really a mind-*heart*-body connection. Prayer should not be just a mental exercise or the performance of a rote ritual. The fire of your heart and your love is what compels the angels to answer your calls. Love is what gives shape to our desires and what should guide our visualizations. So the more heartfelt our prayers are, the more charged they are with spiritual purpose.

Saint Germain talks about this mind-heart-body connection and how the violet flame has been able to help many at deep levels to make both inner and outer progress. In these excerpts, he describes how it has softened the heart and helped heal old hurts:

> The violet flame turns around the downward spiral of the chakras and the negative energy.... The violet flame is the buoyant joy...that turns around spirits and minds and souls and emotions!
>
> (Dec. 2, 1984)

> I should bring to you in this hour a report as to the results of the use of my violet-flame cassettes by one and by the many.[2]
>
> Blessed ones, first and foremost the greatest good has come to the individual supplicant himself. Therefore, to those who have so loved this ritual, there has been an increase of transmutation. And I have seen to it, as you count me as your master and friend, that that violet flame which you have invoked has been directed into the most resistant and recalcitrant pockets of your own subconscious, especially into those conditions which you have

been the most desirous to have removed.

Therefore, in some of you a hearty amount of karma has been balanced, in others hardness of heart has truly melted around the heart chakra. There has come a new love and a new softening, a new compassion, a new sensitivity to life....

The violet flame has assisted in relationships within families. It has served to liberate some to balance old karmas and old hurts and to set individuals on their courses according to their vibration....

It is impossible to enumerate exhaustively all of the benefits of the violet flame but there is indeed an alchemy that does take place within the personality. The violet flame goes after the schisms that cause psychological problems that go back to early childhood and previous incarnations and that have established such deep grooves within the consciousness that in fact they have been difficult to shake lifetime after lifetime....

The violet flame is a considerate flame. It is a loving flame.... It may be difficult to understand how a flame can have consciousness, but remember, a flame is the manifestation of God. A flame is the manifestation of all who have ever served it, even as a mantra embodies the momentum of all who have ever given it....

Blessed ones, I can only say that if you could see what inner progress you have made, you would not cease in the giving of that violet-flame decree tape as often as possible—not necessarily all at once, but if you make the effort, you can endow those segments of time that come to you in the day with your decree momentum on that flame. And therefore, as you should come to understand, whatever time of day you invoke a flame or perform a service it does tie into your karma made at that very same hour throughout history....

In the etheric retreats where you study [as your soul travels out of the body at night], you are shown the filigree thread of light that emits from a heart chakra filled with mercy's love. Some of you have seen where there have been a number of threads so great as to not even be possible of counting, and these threads of violet flame, almost as a gossamer veil, have gone directly to hearts all over the planet.

You have observed these threads, almost as fine as hair, being as vessels, even as veins within the body, carrying a continual flow of violet flame that has enabled individuals all over the world to rise up, to accomplish things they have not accomplished in many lifetimes, to experience hope and healing and a new desire to find God, to be free and to stand for the cause of freedom....

You can in fifteen minutes a day [of giving violet-flame decrees] have me with you; and in my presence with you, you can deliver a momentum of violet flame to many souls upon the planet.

(July 4, 1988)

Creating a Sacred Space

Since spoken prayer is more effective than silent prayer, it is best to give your decrees aloud. If you're in a public place, though, and can't decree aloud, you can repeat the decrees silently. Decrees can be given anywhere, even while you're cleaning the house, doing errands, going for a walk, driving to work, or even taking a shower. It helps, though, when we can set aside some uninterrupted quiet time to decree before our own personal altar.

Your altar is your special place—the sacred space that helps you connect to your heart. It is the place we go when we want to "alter"—to create change and transformation. You can create your own altar, even if it's in a corner of your bedroom or living room.

You can adorn your altar with what is spiritually significant and inspiring to you, like candles, crystals, flowers or plants. You can add pictures or statues of saints, masters, Buddhas or angels as well as photographs of those for whom you are praying. A crystal bowl or goblet can serve as a chalice to focus God's light in your home.

I invite you to experiment with the violet-flame decrees in the next chapter and see what happens. It is my prayer that the sweet people of the world will come together with open hearts and, with a spirit of joy and a vision of hope, give violet-flame decrees. I, for one, would do this simply out of gratitude to Saint Germain, who has continued to work with our souls at great personal sacrifice for thousands of years.

The future is truly in our hands. Our choices now and in the next few years will make all the difference for generations to come.

15 Prayers and Meditations

We are all here on earth to help others,
what on earth the others are here for
I don't know. —W. H. AUDEN

In this chapter, we offer specific prayers, affirmations and decrees you can use to bring spiritual solutions to the prophesied challenges of our time. We have also included suggested visualizations and meditations that can enhance your spiritual practice and help you fulfill your unique purpose in life.

An effective exercise to start your day with is the "Heart, Head and Hand Decrees." This set of affirmations helps purify and energize heart, head and hand for a greater mind-heart-body connection.

The heart is the place where we commune with

God. It is the center from which we send out our love to nourish mankind. Our head is the chalice where we receive the creative thoughts of God and our Higher Self. Our hands represent how we put our spirituality into practice. All three—heart, head and hand—are an integral part of our spirituality.

Heart, Head and Hand

We begin with the heart because the heart is the hub of life, physically and spiritually. With the "Heart" mantra (page 338), we call forth the transmutative power of the violet flame. Layer by layer, the violet flame can dissolve negative feelings and karma that block the flow of energy through the heart. The "Heart" mantra helps us develop the qualities of the heart. It helps us become more open, more sensitive and more compassionate to the plight of so many who need our love and our prayers.

The "Head" mantra clears the physical and spiritual faculties of the mind so that we can think and communicate more clearly. It helps us strengthen our intuitive faculties and develop a keener perception to spiritual dimensions.

In the "Hand" mantra we affirm our partnership with Spirit and we say, "When I join hands with God, nothing will be impossible." The hand symbolizes the power of God to make things happen—through our profession, our service to life, the big and small things we do for others every day. Through our hand we can transfer tremendous energy and healing.

With the "Hand" mantra we also affirm that we will walk the "Middle Way," as Gautama Buddha taught his followers. After his own experimentation, Gautama said the best way to make spiritual progress is to live a balanced life, not succumbing to the extremes of asceticism or indulgence.

Visualization and Meditation:

As you recite the "Heart" mantra, visualize the violet flame within your heart as a pulsating violet light that softens your heart and allows the petals of your heart chakra to open. See the violet flame transforming anger into compassion, bitterness into sweetness, anxiety into peace.

As you give the "Head" mantra, see the violet flame leaping up from your heart and penetrating into your head to clear your mind of all mental blocks, negative images and limiting concepts about yourself or others. See your mind becoming filled with the brilliant light of God.

As you give the "Hand" mantra, visualize the violet flame dissolving the cause, effect, record and memory of those things you had a "hand" in that you wish you had not done. You can give each section below three times, or as many times as you wish.

Heart

Violet fire, thou love divine,
Blaze within this heart of mine!
Thou art mercy forever true,
Keep me always in tune with you.

Head

I AM light, thou Christ in me,
Set my mind forever free;
Violet fire, forever shine
Deep within this mind of mine.

God who gives my daily bread,
With violet fire fill my head
Till thy radiance heavenlike
Makes my mind a mind of light.

Hand

I AM the hand of God in action,
Gaining victory every day;
My pure soul's great satisfaction
Is to walk the Middle Way.

The White Light

The next set of affirmations reinforces our protective "tube of light," shown in the Chart of Your Divine Self (page 315). The tube of light is a shield of protective white light about nine feet in diameter that streams down from God and the I AM THAT I AM above you and extends beneath your feet.

The tube of light can guard against energies of malice that may be directed at you through someone's anger, condemnation, hatred or jealousy. When you are unprotected, those vibrations can make you irritable or depressed. They can even cause you to have accidents.

The white light can also protect you from the pull of the mass consciousness. When we feel exhausted after a trip into the city or after we go shopping during the holiday rush, it's often because our light has been drained. The tube of light helps us stay centered and at peace.

It's a good idea to give your "Tube of Light" decree each morning before the hustle and bustle of the day begins. If throughout the day you feel de-energized, depleted or vulnerable, you can repeat this decree as needed. "The tube of light is invincible," says Saint Germain. "Reinforce it after you have been for a while midst many people and in the commercial world. Withdraw for a few minutes. Reestablish the fire!"

Visualization and Meditation:

As you recite the "Tube of Light" decree, see the dazzling white light from your I AM Presence, brighter than the sun shining on new-fallen snow, coalescing to form an impenetrable wall of light around you. Inside this scintillating tube of light, see yourself enfolded with the violet flame. From time to time throughout the day, you can reinforce this spiritual protection by visualizing the tube of light around you and repeating the decree.

Tube of Light

Beloved I AM Presence bright,
Round me seal your tube of light
From ascended master flame
Called forth now in God's own name.
Let it keep my temple free
From all discord sent to me.

I AM calling forth violet fire
To blaze and transmute all desire,
Keeping on in freedom's name
Till I AM one with the violet flame.

Forgiveness

The next decree is for forgiveness. The violet flame is a forgiving flame. Forgiveness is not always easy, but without forgiveness we cannot make spiritual progress. When we refuse to forgive a friend or a supposed enemy who has wronged us, even if he wrongs us again and again, we tie ourselves not only to that person but to his anger. Therefore, we are not truly free until we resolve the anger and balance the karma.

There may be times when we feel we cannot forgive someone because we believe the crime they committed against us or a loved one has been too great. In a situation like this, God has taught me that we should forgive the soul and ask God to bind the not-self of the person that caused him to commit the crime. No matter how bad a person's deeds are, we should always forgive the soul, thereby avoiding a karmic entanglement. Hatred binds; love frees.

Spiritually speaking, each time we don't forgive someone, we are putting a barrier between ourselves and another part of God. And sometimes the most important person you have to forgive is yourself.

Visualization and Meditation:

As you give the "Forgiveness" mantra, send your love and forgiveness to all whom you have ever wronged and all who have ever wronged you, releasing the situations into God's hands.

Forgiveness

I AM forgiveness acting here,
Casting out all doubt and fear,
Setting men forever free
With wings of cosmic victory.

I AM calling in full power
For forgiveness every hour;
To all life in every place
I flood forth forgiving grace.

The Light of the Heart

Many spiritual traditions tell us that the heart should be the centerpiece of our spirituality. Saint Germain has written a beautiful prayer called "I AM the Light of the Heart" to celebrate the divine flame within our hearts and to help us become heart-centered. He says:

Your heart is indeed one of the choicest gifts of God. Within it there is a central chamber surrounded by such light and protection as that which we call a "cosmic interval." It is a chamber separated from matter, and no probing could ever discover it.

It occupies simultaneously not only the third

and fourth dimensions but also other dimensions unknown to man. It is thus the connecting point of the mighty silver cord of light that descends from your divine God Presence to sustain the beating of your physical heart, giving you life, purpose and cosmic integration.

I urge all to treasure this point of contact that they have with life by paying conscious recognition to it. You do not need to understand by sophisticated language or scientific postulation the how, why and wherefore of this activity.

Be content to know that God is there and that there is within you a point of contact with the Divine, a spark of fire from the Creator's own heart which is called the threefold flame of life. There it burns as the triune essence of love, wisdom and power.

Each acknowledgment paid daily to the flame within your heart will amplify the power and illumination of love within your being. Each such attention will produce a new sense of dimension for you, if not outwardly apparent then subconsciously manifest within the folds of your inner thoughts.

Neglect not, then, your heart as the altar of God. Neglect it not as the sun of your manifest being. Draw from God the power of love and amplify it within your heart. Then send it out into the world at large as the bulwark of that which shall overcome the darkness of the planet....

Remember that as long as you face the light, the shadows are always behind. And the light is there, too, to transmute them all.   (Feb. 12, 1967)

Visualization and Meditation:

As you recite "I AM the Light of the Heart," visualize light descending from your I AM Presence and Holy Christ Self to your heart, where it will be released according to the worded matrix of your decree.

Then center your attention on your heart. Picture the brilliance of the sun at noonday and transfer that picture to the center of your chest, where your heart chakra is located.

Now see thousands of sunbeams going forth from your heart to penetrate and dissolve any darkness, despair or depression first within yourself and then within the people of the world.

Project your love (which is really God's love) out into the world. See that love as intense fiery-pink laser beams that break down all barriers to the success of your relationships, your family, your spiritual growth, your career, your neighborhood or your nation.

I AM the Light of the Heart

I AM the light of the heart
Shining in the darkness of being
And changing all into the golden treasury
Of the mind of Christ.

I AM projecting my love
Out into the world
To erase all errors
And to break down all barriers.

I AM the power of infinite love,
Amplifying itself
Until it is victorious,
World without end!

Saint Germain's Mantra for the Aquarian Age

The affirmation Saint Germain has given us for the Aquarian age is "I AM a being of violet fire! I AM the purity God desires!" Remember, this really means "God in me is a being of violet fire! God in me is the purity God desires!"

You can repeat this affirmation over and over again as a mantra that sings in your heart. As you give it, visualize dancing violet flames consuming negative karma and habit patterns that hinder you or those you pray for. You can create your own variations on the theme, wherever you perceive a need, such as:

I AM a being of violet fire!
I AM the purity God desires!

My heart is alive with violet fire!
My heart is the purity God desires!

My family is enfolded in violet fire!
My family is the purity God desires!

Earth is a planet of violet fire!
Earth is the purity God desires!

"I AM the Violet Flame"

"I AM the Violet Flame" is a powerful decree that you can repeat many times to build a strong action of transmutation.

Visualization and Meditation:

See the violet flame come to life as if you were looking at a movie. The flames rise and pulsate around you in different shades and gradations of purple, pink and violet.

See these flames pass through your body, caressing each organ and restoring wholeness. See them saturating your mind and your emotions, relieving all burdens.

One of my favorite visualizations for this decree is to see the seven seas filled with violet flame. Meditate on the power of the seven seas and then translate that image into a giant, peaceful violet-flame sea that envelops the entire planet. Imagine the weight of it, the power of it, the energy of it. The violet flame has the capacity to totally transform the earth, the air and the waters.

You can apply this decree to specific situations. You can see the violet flame transmuting the pollution in a local river or clearing the smog over your city. You can focus on the world's children. Visualize them before you, starting with the children of your own neighborhood and moving on to the needy children of the world. See frolicking, dancing violet flames swaddling them and transforming their burdens into joy.

I AM the Violet Flame

I AM the violet flame
  In action in me now
I AM the violet flame
  To Light alone I bow
I AM the violet flame
  In mighty cosmic power
I AM the light of God
  Shining every hour
I AM the violet flame
  Blazing like a sun
I AM God's sacred power
  Freeing every one

Purifying and Energizing Your Chakras

Sometimes we don't immediately feel the action of the light we call forth in our decrees. This is because our auras or our chakras (spiritual centers) may be clogged.

Your chakras are receiving and sending stations for the energy of God that flows to you and from you each day. They are gateways to higher consciousness.

Situated along your spinal column at spiritual levels, they are invisible to the physical eye. Yet your very life and spiritual progress depend on their vitality.

Chakra is a Sanskrit term meaning "wheel" or "disc." Each chakra has a unique function and frequency and represents a different level of consciousness. These differences are denoted by the number of "petals" of each chakra. The more petals the chakra has, the higher its frequency. And the more energy that flows through a chakra, the faster it spins.

As the light of the Divine Mother, called the Kundalini, rises from the base of the spine to the crown, it activates the energies of each chakra. As that chakra begins to spin, it opens and raises its petals, signifying the unfoldment of our latent spiritual powers.

Unfortunately, by our interactions with others throughout our many incarnations, karmic debris has accumulated around our chakras. This debris is like the leaves that clog up a drain after it has rained. In order for the water to run through the drain properly, we need to clear away the leaves. Likewise, in order for God's light to flow through and activate our chakras, we need to clear the effluvia that clings to these sacred centers.

When our chakras are clogged, we can feel sluggish, pessimistic or sick without even knowing why. When our chakras and the circuits of energy that connect them are clear, we feel more energetic, positive, joyful and giving.

I've seen thousands of people work successfully with the violet flame to clear their chakras. It takes a different amount of time—anywhere from a day to several months—for each person to see results. But if you remain constant, you will begin to feel the difference. I always recommend to those who are new to the violet flame that they experiment with it. I tell them to give violet-flame decrees for at least a month, fifteen minutes a day, and to note the positive changes that start to take place in their life.

You can use any of the violet-flame decrees in this chapter, especially the following affirmations, to purify and energize your chakras so that you can experience the highest levels of your spiritual potential. This set of affirmations starts with the central chakra, the heart chakra, and moves in a spiral action through the chakras above and below the heart. Give each set of affirmations three times or in multiples of three.

Chakra Affirmations

I AM a being of violet fire!
I AM the purity God desires!

My heart is a chakra of violet fire,
My heart is the purity God desires!

I AM a being of violet fire!
I AM the purity God desires!

My throat chakra is a wheel of violet fire,
My throat chakra is the purity God desires!

I AM a being of violet fire!
I AM the purity God desires!

My solar plexus is a sun of violet fire,
My solar plexus is the purity God desires!

I AM a being of violet fire!
I AM the purity God desires!

My third eye is a center of violet fire,
My third eye is the purity God desires!

I AM a being of violet fire!
I AM the purity God desires!

My soul chakra is a sphere of violet fire,
My soul is the purity God desires!

I AM a being of violet fire!
I AM the purity God desires!

My crown chakra is a lotus of violet fire,
My crown chakra is the purity God desires!

I AM a being of violet fire!
I AM the purity God desires!

> My base chakra is a fount of violet fire,
> My base chakra is the purity God desires!
>
> I AM a being of violet fire!
> I AM the purity God desires!

Visualization and Meditation:

The following meditation is for clearing the chakras. It works well to give it either before, during or after you give the preceding chakra affirmations.

First, see the violet flame bathing and cleansing all your chakras as it flows up and down your spinal column. See the flames dissolve the debris that has collected around your chakras.

Then see your heart chakra, twelve-petaled, a fiery rose pink, sending the light of divine love to all sentient life.

See your throat chakra, sixteen-petaled, a fiery blue sapphire, sending the light of God's will to all nations and peoples.

See your solar-plexus chakra, ten-petaled, purple and gold with ruby flecks, sending the light of peace and brotherhood to harmonize all life.

See your third eye, ninety-six-petaled, a fiery emerald green, sending the light of God's vision and truth for healing.

See your seat-of-the-soul chakra, six-petaled, violet-purple-pink, sending the violet flame for freedom, forgiveness, justice and world transmutation.

See your crown chakra, thousand-petaled, a brilliant yellow fire, sending the light of wisdom and illumined action to dispel all darkness.

See your base-of-the-spine chakra, four-petaled, pure white, sending God's light to bring joy, hope and wholeness to all souls on earth.

Now visualize the center of each chakra as a fiery sun of white light. Sustain the image of a powerful white ray of light shooting out from the center of each chakra. Once you have visualized these rays with intensity, one by one see each white ray wrapped in a cylinder that is the color of that chakra.

Prayers for the Nature Spirits

Here are some prayers and decrees you can give on behalf of the nature spirits (elementals), whose plight we described in chapter 7.

In the name of the I AM THAT I AM, I call forth the intense action of the violet transmuting flame around every gnome, sylph, undine and salamander. Saturate the four elements—fire, air, water and earth— with the violet flame this day!

Consume the cause and core of mankind's karma that is a burden upon the nature spirits. Transmute the poisons and toxins—at physical, emotional, mental and etheric levels—that pollute our earth.

Charge the violet flame into the earth, into the waters, into the atmosphere, and into the very nucleus of fire in every atom of life!

(Repeat each decree three times or in multiples of three:)

The nature spirits are beings of violet fire!
The nature spirits are the purity God desires! (3x)

O violet flame, come, violet flame,
Now blaze and blaze and blaze!
O violet flame, come, violet flame,
To raise and raise and raise!
The air, the sea, the land
The air, the sea, the land
The air, the sea, the land. (3x)

Seal, seal, seal in an ovoid bright
Of the violet fire's clear light
Every elemental, set and keep them free
From all human discord instantly.
It's done today, it's done to stay,
it's done God's way. (3x)

I AM, I AM, I AM the resurrection and the life
of all elementals—fire, air, water and earth! (3x)

Transmuting World Karma

Astrology is the signature of our returning karma and therefore can be used to chart our coming challenges and opportunities. You can offer the following prayer by itself or preceding any violet-flame decree to (1) transmute your personal karma and (2) transmute world karma that could result in the astrological portents I discussed in chapters 1, 4 and 5.

Prayer for the Transmutation
of Astrological Portents

Beloved mighty victorious Presence of God, I AM in me, my very own beloved Holy Christ Self, Holy Christ Selves of all mankind, Saint Germain, Mother Mary and the seven archangels, direct the violet flame into all positive and negative portents of my personal astrology for the maximum balancing of my karma.

I call for the light of God to seal my astrological chart in every level and in every aspect, releasing only the light of God. I call for the transmutation of the karma that would magnetize and make me vulnerable to planetary and interplanetary forces. I call for the transmutation and elimination of the momentums that created my karma and my negative human habit patterns.

I also call for the binding, sealing, demagnetization, neutralization and transmutation of the negative effects of personal and world karma that could manifest through the portents of the May 3, 2000 megaconjunction in Taurus, transiting Pluto in Sagittarius and Capricorn, transiting Uranus in Aquarius and Pisces, and transiting Neptune in Aquarius and Pisces, including but not limited to:

national, religious and cultural conflict; tyranny, war, revolution or terrorism; repression of new ideas and a stifling of the human spirit; persecution along class, religious and ethnic lines;

the misuse of science and technology; the dividing of society into an elite of technological haves and an underclass of technological have-nots; confusion, disillusionment and anarchy; bitterness and resentment;

new, widespread forms of escapism; intense power struggles; nuclear war, nuclear accidents or nuclear terrorism; uncontrolled mass movements; physical or social earthquakes and earth changes; epidemics and depressed immune response.

I also call for the manifestation of the positive potential of these configurations, including:

The birth of a golden age of enlightenment, transcendent spirituality and brotherhood; a positive transformation in the vision we hold of ourselves, our world, our place in the universe and our relationship to God; self-transcendence and a practical expression of spirituality;

technological advances; optimism, expansion and innovation; solutions to social problems and the dissolution of barriers that divide people by religion, race, nationality, class and gender;

the development of innovative forms of service to mankind; advances in medicine, education and the dissemination of information; the advancement of mankind due to a revolution in science and the commensurate spiritual revolution that will guide the wise use of these powers.

(Follow with your choice of violet-flame decrees)

16 A Rosary for World Peace

You have forgotten that through
prayer and fasting you can avert
war and suspend the laws of nature.
—MARY TO THE MEDJUGORJE SEERS

In her many appearances throughout the world, Mother Mary has stressed that prayer and the recitation of the rosary are keys to lasting world peace. She has created the following non-denominational rosary that can be given by people of all faiths.

As we join together in this universal prayer for peace, Mary promises to help us resolve personal difficulties as well as overcome world challenges. The rosary is also a gentle way to raise the Kunda-lini (Mother light) through the chakras for greater spiritual awareness.

This rosary alternates prayers with passages from I Corinthians 13 and 14 on the virtue of charity (love). Each time we give the rosary, says Mary, we are building a momentum of light and love that can spiritually buoy up those in need. She says the rosary can literally work miracles in turning back the negative portents of prophecy:

> I live with the Fátima prophecy. I live with its message. And I go from door to door and heart to heart knocking, asking for those who will come and pray with me—pray the violet flame or the rosary or the calls to Archangel Michael. But above all, pray. For by thy prayer is the open door extended, and the angels come stepping through the veil to prevent disaster and calamity.

Rosary for World Peace

In the name of the Father and of the Son and of the Holy Spirit, in the name of the Cosmic Virgin, Amen.

The Keeper's Daily Prayer

A flame is active—
A flame is vital—
A flame is eternal.

I AM a God flame of radiant love
From the very heart of God
In the Great Central Sun,
Descending from the Master of Life!
I AM charged now
With beloved Helios and Vesta's
Supreme God consciousness
And solar awareness.

Pilgrim upon earth,
I AM walking daily the way
Of the ascended masters' victory
That leads to my eternal freedom
By the power of the sacred fire
This day and always,
Continually made manifest
In my thoughts, feelings, and immediate awareness,
Transcending and transmuting

All the elements of earth
Within my four lower bodies
And freeing me by the power of the sacred fire
From those misqualified foci of energy
   within my being.

I AM set free right now from all that binds
By and through the currents of the divine flame
Of the sacred fire itself,
Whose ascending action makes me
God in manifestation,
God in action,
God by direction and
God in consciousness!

I AM an active flame!
I AM a vital flame!
I AM an eternal flame!
I AM an expanding fire spark
From the Great Central Sun
Drawing to me now every ray
Of divine energy which I need
And which can never be requalified by the human
And flooding me with the light
And God-illumination of a thousand suns
To take dominion and rule supreme forever
Everywhere I AM!

Where I AM, there God is also.
Unseparated forever I remain,
Increasing my light
By the smile of his radiance,
The fullness of his love,
The omniscience of his wisdom,
And the power of his life eternal,
Which automatically raises me
On ascension's wings of victory
That shall return me to the heart of God
From whence in truth
I AM come to do God's will
And manifest abundant life to all!

Call to the Fire Breath

I AM, I AM, I AM the fire breath of God
From the heart of beloved Alpha and Omega.
This day I AM the immaculate concept
In expression everywhere I move.
Now I AM full of joy,
For now I AM the full expression
Of divine love.

My beloved I AM Presence,
Seal me now within the very heart
Of the expanding fire breath of God.
Let its purity, wholeness and love
Manifest everywhere I AM today and forever!

I accept this done right now with full power!
I AM this done right now with full power!
I AM, I AM, I AM God-life expressing
Perfection all ways at all times.
This which I call forth for myself
I call forth for every man, woman,
and child on this planet.

I AM Lord's Prayer
by Jesus the Christ

Our Father who art in heaven,
Hallowed be thy name, I AM.
I AM thy kingdom come
I AM thy will being done
I AM on earth even as I AM in heaven
I AM giving this day daily bread to all
I AM forgiving all life this day even as
I AM also all life forgiving me
I AM leading all men away from temptation
I AM delivering all men from
    every evil condition
I AM the kingdom
I AM the power and
I AM the glory of God in eternal,
    immortal manifestation—
All this I AM.

Though I speak with the tongues of men and of angels and have not charity, I am become as sounding brass or a tinkling cymbal.

Hail Mary

Hail, Mary, full of grace
the Lord is with thee.
Blessed art thou among women
and blessed is the fruit of thy womb, Jesus.
Holy Mary, Mother of God,
Pray for us, sons and daughters of God,
Now and at the hour of our victory
Over sin, disease and death.

And though I have the gift of prophecy and understand all mysteries and all knowledge, and though I have all faith so that I could remove mountains and have not charity, I am nothing.

Give the Hail Mary

And though I bestow all my goods to feed the poor, and though I give my body to be burned, and have not charity, it profiteth me nothing.

Give the Hail Mary

Charity suffereth long, and is kind; charity envieth not; charity vaunteth not itself, is not puffed up,

Give the Hail Mary

Doth not behave itself unseemly, seeketh not her own, is not easily provoked, thinketh no evil;

Give the Hail Mary

Rejoiceth not in iniquity, but rejoiceth in the truth;

Give the Hail Mary

Beareth all things, believeth all things, hopeth all things, endureth all things.

Give the Hail Mary

Give the I AM Lord's Prayer

Charity never faileth, but whether there be prophecies, they shall fail; whether there be tongues, they shall cease; whether there be knowledge, it shall vanish away.

Give the Hail Mary

For we know in part and we prophesy in part. But when that which is perfect is come, then that which is in part shall be done away.

Give the Hail Mary

When I was a child, I spake as a child, I understood as a child, I thought as a child: but when I became a man, I put away childish things.

Give the Hail Mary

For now we see through a glass, darkly, but then face to face. Now I know in part, but then shall I know even as also I am known.

Give the Hail Mary

And now abideth faith, hope, charity, these three; but the greatest of these is charity.

Give the Hail Mary

Follow after charity and desire spiritual gifts, but rather that ye may prophesy.

Give the Hail Mary

For he that speaketh in an unknown tongue speaketh not unto men but unto God, for no man understandeth him, howbeit in the spirit he speaketh mysteries.

Give the Hail Mary

Give the I AM Lord's Prayer

But he that prophesieth speaketh unto men to edification and exhortation and comfort.

Give the Hail Mary

He that speaketh in an unknown tongue edifieth himself, but he that prophesieth edifieth the church.

Give the Hail Mary

I would that ye all spake with tongues, but rather that ye prophesied: for greater is he that prophesieth than he that speaketh with tongues, except he interpret, that the church may receive edifying.

Give the Hail Mary

Now, brethren, if I come unto you speaking with tongues, what shall I profit you, except I shall speak to you either by revelation, or by knowledge, or by prophesying, or by doctrine?

Give the Hail Mary

And even things without life giving sound, whether pipe or harp, except they give a distinction in the sounds, how shall it be known what is piped or harped?

Give the Hail Mary

For if the trumpet give an uncertain sound, who shall prepare himself to the battle?

Give the Hail Mary

So likewise ye, except ye utter by the tongue words easy to be understood, how shall it be known what is spoken? for ye shall speak into the air.

Give the Hail Mary

Transfiguring Affirmations
of Jesus the Christ

I AM THAT I AM

I AM the open door which no man can shut

I AM the light which lighteth every man
that cometh into the world

I AM the way

I AM the truth

I AM the life

I AM the resurrection

I AM the ascension in the light

I AM the fulfillment of all my needs and
requirements of the hour

I AM abundant supply[1] poured out upon all life

I AM perfect sight and hearing

I AM the manifest perfection of being

I AM the illimitable light of God
made manifest everywhere

I AM the light of the holy of holies

I AM a son of God

I AM the light in the holy mountain of God

Glory Be to the Father

Glory be to the Father
and to the Son
and to the Holy Spirit!
As it was in the beginning,
is now and ever shall be,
life without end—
I AM, I AM, I AM!

In the name of the Father and of the Son and of the Holy Spirit, in the name of the Cosmic Virgin, Amen.

In the Immaculate Heart of Mary, I trust.
In the Immaculate Heart of Mary, I trust.
In the Immaculate Heart of Mary, I trust.

Notes

Chapter 1
A Sneak Preview

1. See Elizabeth Clare Prophet, *Fallen Angels and the Origins of Evil: Why Church Fathers Suppressed the Book of Enoch and Its Startling Revelations* (Corwin Springs, Mont.: Summit University Press, 2000).

2. Quotes from the Book of Jonah are taken from the Jerusalem Bible.

3. See *The Opus Majus of Roger Bacon,* trans. Robert Belle Burke, vol. 1 (Philadelphia: University of Pennsylvania Press, 1928), pp. 400–401.

4. See Samuel P. Huntington, *The Clash of Civilizations and the Remaking of World Order;* and Panel Discussion, "Pluto in Sagittarius," *The Mountain Astrologer,* July 1995, p. 13.

5. Laurie A. Baum, *Astrological Secrets for the New Millennium* (Rocklin, Calif.: Prima Publishing, 1997), p. 96.

Chapter 2
Nostradamus: Seer of the Centuries

1. Date based on the Julian calendar. December 23 by the Gregorian calendar.

2. Century I, quatrain 63, in Edgar Leoni, *Nostradamus and His Prophecies* (New York: Bell Publishing Co., 1961), p. 149.

3. Stewart Robb, *Prophecies on World Events by Nostradamus* (New York: Ace Books, 1961), p. 119.

4. Stewart Robb, *Nostradamus and the End of Evils Begun* (Santa Ana, Calif.: Parca Publishing Co., 1984), p. 20.

5. Robb, *Prophecies,* p. 59.

6. Ibid., p. 60.

7. Stewart Robb believes that Nostradamus is referring to the "War of the Three Henrys" (1585). See Century VI, quatrain 2, in Robb, *Prophecies,* p. 50; Erika Cheetham, *The Prophecies of Nostradamus* (New York: Berkley Books, 1973), p. 250.

8. Leoni, *Nostradamus,* p. 341.

9. Ibid., p. 690.

10. Ibid., p. 339.

11. Robb, *Prophecies,* p. 21.

12. Ibid., pp. 24–25.

13. Ibid., pp. 23–24.

14. Ibid., pp. 18, 42, 64, 129, 133; Leoni, *Nostradamus,* pp. 169, 589; Stewart Robb, *Nostradamus on Napoleon* (New York: Oracle Press, 1961).

15. Leoni, *Nostradamus,* pp. 57, 58.

16. Ibid., p. 141.

17. Jean Héritier, *Catherine de Medici,* trans. Charlotte Haldane (London: George Allen & Unwin, 1963), p. 77.

18. Jean-Charles de Fontbrune, *Nostradamus 2: Into the Twenty-First Century,* trans. Alexis Lykiard (London: Pan Books, 1986), p. 22.

19. Leoni, *Nostradamus,* p. 133.

20. Ibid., p. 103.

21. Ibid., p. 329.

22. Century III, quatrain 55, in Cheetham, *Prophecies of Nostradamus,* p. 144.

23. Lee McCann, *Nostradamus: The Man Who Saw through Time* (New York: Farrar, Straus and Giroux, 1941), p. 155.

24. Leoni, *Nostradamus,* pp. 112, 327, 329.

Chapter 3
A Time of Peace or a Time of War?

1. Epistle to Henry II, in Leoni, *Nostradamus,* p. 345.

2. Ibid., p. 187.

3. See Rev. 1:13–16.

4. Leoni, *Nostradamus,* p. 253.

5. Ibid., p. 149.

6. Edward Teller and Allen Brown, *The Legacy of Hiroshima* (Garden City, N.Y.: Doubleday & Co., 1962), p. 5.

7. Michael Pogodzinski, *Second Sunrise—Nuclear War: The Untold Story* (Thorndike, Maine: Thorndike Press, 1983), p. 97.

8. Erika Cheetham, *The Further Prophecies of Nostradamus: 1985 and Beyond* (New York: Putnam Publishing Group, Perigee Books, 1985), p. 96.

9. Leoni, *Nostradamus,* p. 397.

10. See John Hogue, *Nostradamus: The Complete Prophecies* (Shaftesbury, Dorset: Element Books, 1997), pp. 727–29; Erika Cheetham, *The Final Prophecies of Nostradamus* (New York: Putnam Publishing Group, Perigee Books, 1989), p. 380; Peter Lemesurier, *Nostradamus: The Next 50 Years* (New York: Berkley Publishing Group, Berkley Books, 1994), pp. 181–82.

11. Leoni, *Nostradamus,* p. 309.

12. Cheetham, *Further Prophecies of Nostradamus,* pp. 194–95.

13. "Fears Mount over Millennium Bombs," Dec. 6, MSNBC.com/news/220749.asp.

14. Robb, *Nostradamus and the End of Evils Begun,* p. 137.

15. Ibid., p. 49.

16. Leoni, *Nostradamus,* p. 657.

17. Cheetham, *Final Prophecies of Nostradamus,* p. 263.

18. Rene Noorbergen, *Nostradamus Predicts the End of the World* (New York: Pinnacle Books, 1982), p. 49.

19. Cheetham, *Final Prophecies of Nostradamus*, p. 263.

20. Hogue, *Nostradamus: Complete Prophecies*, p. 442.

21. Robb, *Nostradamus and the End of Evils Begun*, p. 51.

22. Leoni, *Nostradamus*, p. 149.

23. Cheetham, *Further Prophecies of Nostradamus*, p. 95.

24. Epistle to Henry II, in Leoni, *Nostradamus*, p. 345.

25. Hogue, *Nostradamus: Complete Prophecies*, p. 617.

26. Leoni, *Nostradamus*, p. 401.

27. Ibid., p. 287.

28. See Hogue, *Nostradamus: Complete Prophecies*, p. 454; Cheetham, *Prophecies of Nostradamus*, p. 258.

29. Cheetham, *Final Prophecies of Nostradamus*, p. 271.

30. John Hogue, *Nostradamus: The New Revelations* (Shaftesbury, Dorset: Element Books, 1994), p. 248.

Chapter 4
A Parable for Our Time

1. Leoni, *Nostradamus*, p. 435.

2. Ibid., p. 750.

3. "Saddam + Bin Laden," *Newsweek*, 11 January 1999.

4. Lemesurier, *Nostradamus: Next Fifty Years*, pp. 2, 74, 286. According to Lemesurier, the apostrophe in *d'effraieur* (which has caused this phrase to be commonly translated as "of terror") was not in the earliest editions of Nostradamus' quatrains but does appear in later corrupt editions.

5. See Goro Adachi's site on the Internet:

prophetic.simplenet.com

6. Hogue, *Nostradamus: Complete Prophecies*, p. 800.
7. Nostradamus, Preface, in Leoni, *Nostradamus*, p. 127.
8. This refers to the "conceptional chart" of the United States. We consider that there are separate charts for the conception and birth of the United States. Many astrologers assume that the United States was born on July 4, 1776, the day the Declaration of Independence was signed. We see the signing of the Declaration of Independence as the moment that the United States was conceived—July 4, 1776, 5:13 p.m. We consider April 30, 1789, as the birth of the United States. That was the day George Washington was sworn in as president.

Chapter 5
The Handwriting in the Skies

1. A progressed chart is calculated by advancing (or "progressing") the positions of the planets, Ascendant and the Midheaven. They are progressed at the rate of one day's movement for each year from birth. Progressed charts are used to assess influences any time after the birth of a person, corporation, nation, etc.
2. See note 8 above.
3. Robert Gates and Richard Kerr, quoted in "World 'Close' to Nuclear War in '90," *The Arizona Republic*, 22 March 1993, p. A12.

Chapter 6
Nostradamus & Cayce on Earth Changes

1. Leoni, *Nostradamus,* p. 427.
2. Ibid., p. 157. Most commentators translate the first word of the quatrain, *ennosigée,* as "earth-shaking." In Leoni's translation it is "volcanic."
3. Hogue, *Nostradamus: Complete Prophecies,* p. 138.
4. Lemesurier, *Nostradamus: Next Fifty Years,* p. 172.
5. Noorbergen, *Nostradamus Predicts the End of the World,* pp. 160–62.
6. Rev. 16:18, 19.
7. Hugh Lynn Cayce, *Earth Changes Update* (Virginia Beach, Va.: A.R.E. Press, 1980), pp. 87, 89–90.
8. William Hutton, *Coming Earth Changes: Causes and Consequences of the Approaching Pole Shift* (Virginia Beach, Va.: A.R.E. Press, 1996), p. 99.
9. Hugh Lynn Cayce, *Earth Changes Update,* pp. 91–92.
10. Hutton, *Coming Earth Changes,* pp. 200–201, 203.
11. Hugh Lynn Cayce, *Earth Changes Update,* p. 104.
12. Edgar Cayce, quoted in Hutton, *Coming Earth Changes,* p. 23.
13. Edgar Cayce, Reading #5757-1.
14. Hugh Lynn Cayce, *Earth Changes Update,* pp. 106, 105.
15. Jess Stearn, *Edgar Cayce on the Millennium* (New York: Warner Books, 1998), p. 192.
16. Edgar Cayce, quoted in Hugh Lynn Cayce, *Earth*

Changes Update, p. 106.

17. Mary Ellen Carter, *Edgar Cayce on Prophecy* (New York: Warner Books, 1968), p. 55; and Stearn, *Edgar Cayce on the Millennium,* p. 92.

18. Stearn, *Edgar Cayce on the Millennium* (New York: Warner Books, 1998), p. 93.

19. Hugh Lynn Cayce, *Earth Changes Update,* p. 30.

20. Ibid., pp. 39, 30.

21. Carter, *Edgar Cayce on Prophecy,* p. 31.

22. Edgar Cayce, Reading #3976-18.

23. Carter, *Edgar Cayce on Prophecy,* p. 35.

24. Hugh Lynn Cayce, *Earth Changes Update,* p. 37.

25. Ibid., p. 30.

26. Ibid., pp. 107–8.

27. Ibid., p. 25.

28. Ibid., p. 106.

Chapter 7
Is Mother Nature Mad?

1. From a study by Worldwatch Institute, an environmental research group, and Munich Re, the world's largest reinsurer.

2. "Humans Blamed for Record Year," *Bozeman Daily Chronicle,* 28 November 1998.

3. Ibid.

4. Notebook, *Time,* 1 June 1998.

5. Peter Tompkins, *The Secret Life of Nature: Living in Harmony with the Hidden World of Nature*

Spirits from Fairies to Quarks (HarperSanFrancisco, 1997), p. 2.

6. Ibid., p. 1.
7. Ibid., pp. 1–2.
8. Ibid., p. 2.
9. Ibid., pp. 16–17.
10. Matt. 7:2.
11. *Akasha* is primary substance, the subtlest, ethereal essence, which fills the whole of space. All that transpires in an individual's world and all events in the physical universe are recorded in *akasha*. These recordings can be read by those with developed soul faculties.

Chapter 8
Passing through the Eye of the Needle

1. Rev. 1:1.
2. Rev. 6:5, 6.
3. Rev. 6:1, 2.
4. Rev. 6:3, 4.
5. Rom. 7:19.
6. Rev. 6:7, 8.
7. I Cor. 3:16.
8. John 14:30.

Chapter 9
The Queen of Angels Reaches Out

1. *Fatima in Lucia's Own Words: Sister Lucia's Memoirs*, ed. Louis Kondor (Fatima, Portugal: Postula-

tion Centre, distributed by Ravengate Press), p. 62.

2. William C. McGrath, "The Lady of the Rosary," in *A Woman Clothed with the Sun,* ed. John J. Delaney (Garden City, N.Y.: Doubleday & Company, Image Books, 1961), p. 182.

3. William Thomas Walsh, *Our Lady of Fátima* (Garden City, N.Y.: Doubleday & Company, Image Books, 1954), p. 220.

4. Ibid., p. 221.

5. McGrath, "Lady of the Rosary," p. 193.

6. Ibid., pp. 194–95.

7. *Fatima in Lucia's Own Words,* pp. 198–99.

8. Frère Michel de la Sainte Trinité, *The Whole Truth about Fátima,* vol. 2 (Buffalo, N.Y.: Immaculate Heart Publications, 1989), p. 666.

9. "Sister Lucy Interviewed by Blue Army," *The Fatima Crusader,* no. 33 (summer 1990), p. 13.

10. Christopher Ruddy, "Defector Reveals Russian War Plans," 8 February 1999, NewsMax.com and *The Pittsburgh Tribune-Review.*

11. Frère Michel de la Sainte Trinité, *The Whole Truth about Fatima,* vol. 3 (Buffalo, N.Y.: Immaculate Heart Publications, 1990), p. 661.

12. Frère Michel de la Sainte Trinité, "The Third Secret Revealed..." *The Fatima Crusader,* no. 20 (June–July 1986), p. 21.

13. *Fatima in Lucia's Own Words,* p. 199.

14. Frère Michel, "The Third Secret Revealed...," p. 23.

15. See Matt. 24.

16. Rev. 16:1.

17. Joseph A. Pelletier, *The Queen of Peace Visits Medugorje* (Worcester, Mass.: Assumption Publication, 1985), p. 49.

18. René Laurentin and Ljudevit Rupcic, *Is the Virgin Mary Appearing at Medjugorje?* (Word Among Us Press), appendix 1.

19. Judith M. Albright, *Our Lady of Medjugorje* (Milford, Ohio: Riehle Foundation, 1988), p. 32.

20. Kenneth L. Woodward, "Visitations of the Virgin," *Newsweek*, 20 July 1987, p. 55.

21. "A Letter from Rome on Medjugorje," posted on the official Medjugorje site on the Internet, www.medjugorje.org

22. "Pope John Paul II on Medjugorje," www.medjugorje.org/pope.htm

23. Father Tomislav Vlasic's report to Pope John Paul II, December 1983.

24. "Medjugorje News Notes," *Medjugorje Magazine* 3, no. 3 (July-August-September 1992), pp. 6–7.

25. Wayne Weible, *Miracle at Medjugorje*, March 1987, p. 2.

26. Father Tomislav Vlasic's December 1983 report, in Laurentin and Rupcic, *Is the Virgin Mary Appearing at Medjugorje?* appendix 1; and Pelletier, *Queen of Peace Visits Medugorje*, pp. 138–39.

27. Ibid.

Chapter 10
Mary's Plan for Peace

1. Laurentin and Rupcic, *Is the Virgin Mary Appearing at Medjugorje?* appendix 1; and Pelletier, *Queen of Peace Visits Medugorje,* pp. 149, 230.
2. Francis Johnston, *Fatima: The Great Sign* (Washington, N.J.: AMI Press, 1980), p. 139.
3. Pelletier, *Queen of Peace Visits Medugorje,* p. 227.
4. Ibid., pp. 217, 221; and www.medugorje.org/msg85.htm.
5. V. Montes de Oca, *More about Fatima,* trans. J. DaCruz, rev. ed. (Apostles of Mary), p. 67.
6. *Fatima in Lucia's Own Words,* p. 64.
7. Hundreds of statues of Mother Mary throughout the world have been seen and photographed shedding tears, particularly those known as the Pilgrim Madonna, which bear the likeness of Mary's appearance at Fátima. Observers say that there is a correlation between world events and the weeping of the statues.

Chapter 11
Saint Germain & the Thread of Prophecy

1. The quotes about the Comte de St. Germain in this section are taken from Isabel Cooper-Oakley, *The Count of Saint Germain* (Blauvelt, N.Y.: Rudolf Steiner Publications, 1970).
2. See I Sam. 7.

3. See I Sam. 8.

4. Henry Thomas and Dana Lee Thomas, *Living Biographies of Great Scientists* (Garden City, N.Y.: Nelson Doubleday, 1941), p. 15.

5. Ibid., p. 16.

6. Ibid., p. 20.

7. Francis Bacon's word-cipher was discovered by cryptographer Dr. Orville W. Owen, who published five volumes of *Sir Francis Bacon's Cipher Story* between 1893 and 1895. The story hidden in his word-cipher can be constructed by stringing together words, lines, and passages from the works of various Elizabethan writers. In contrast, deciphering the bi-literal cipher is an exact, scientific process of grouping together the italic letters (printed in two different fonts of type) that appear with peculiar frequency in original editions of the Shakespearean plays and other of Bacon's works. This cipher was discovered by an assistant of Dr. Owen, Mrs. Elizabeth Wells Gallup, who first published the stories Bacon had concealed in his bi-literal cipher in 1899. To insure that his ciphers would eventually be discovered and his true life story revealed, Bacon had described in detail the bi-literal method of cipher writing in his Latin version of *De Augmentis* (1624), which some 270 years later Mrs. Gallup studied and applied. Ironically, Mrs. Gallup found that Bacon's bi-literal cipher contained complete directions on how to construct the

word-cipher, which was actually discovered first by Dr. Owen.

8. Will Durant, *The Story of Philosophy: The Lives and Opinions of the Greater Philosophers* (Garden City, N.Y.: Garden City Publishing Co., 1927), p. 157.

Chapter 12
Prophecy Is Not Set in Stone

1. I Cor. 14:3.
2. See Jer. 7:31; 19; 52.
3. Helen Wambach, *Life before Life* (New York: Bantam Books, 1979), p. 164.

Chapter 13
A High-Frequency Energy

1. Isa. 45:11.
2. Job 22: 27, 28.
3. See Elizabeth Clare Prophet, *How to Work with Angels* (Corwin Springs, Mont.: Summit University Press, 1998).
4. See Elizabeth Clare Prophet, *Creative Power of Sound* (Corwin Springs, Mont.: Summit University Press, 1998).
5. In the past, individuals were required to balance 100 percent of their karma while still in embodiment in order to make their ascension. Under the dispensation of the Aquarian age, individuals may

ascend after balancing 51 percent of their karma and can balance the remaining 49 percent from the heaven-world. For more on the process of the ascension, see Annice Booth, *The Path to Your Ascension: Rediscovering Life's Ultimate Purpose* (Corwin Springs, Mont.: Summit University, 1999).

Chapter 14
The Mind-Body Connection

1. Tim Wilson, "Chant: The Healing Power of Voice and Ear: An Interview with Alfred Tomatis, M.D.," in *Music: Physician for Times to Come,* ed. Don Campbell (Wheaton, Ill.: Theosophical Publishing House, Quest Books, 1991), p. 13.
2. Saint Germain is referring to audiocassettes of violet-flame decrees and affirmations available through Summit University Press.

Chapter 16
A Rosary for World Peace

1. The word *supply* in this prayer refers to spiritual and material prosperity, including all the resources we need to fulfill our life's purpose.

Acknowledgments

We send our heartfelt thanks to Nigel J. Yorwerth for his genius in conceiving the idea for this book and for his inspiration, creativity and marketing skills that helped shape its contents every step along the way. We are grateful to our editor, Karen Gordon, for her infinite care and constancy, unflagging support, and editorial skills that shepherded this book through the eye of the needle.

We would also like to thank the rest of the team who helped fashion and give birth to this book: Roger Gefvert for capturing the spirit and vision of our book in his beautiful cover artwork and design; Susan Mead for her enthusiasm, cheerleading and meticulous research; Lynn Wilbert for her creative graphic design, make-it-happen spirit and joy; and Judith Younger and Virginia Wood for their careful proofing and their sensitive hearts.

Credits

Grateful acknowledgment is made for permission to reproduce the following material:

Excerpts from *The Count of Saint Germain,* by Isabel Cooper-Oakley. Reprinted by permission of The Theosophical Society in England.

Page 179: The three seers of Fátima. Courtesy of Missions Consolata Publications, Fátima, Portugal.

Page 191: The six seers of Medjugorje. Courtesy of the original Center for Peace, Boston, Massachusetts.

Every effort has been made to ensure that all necessary permissions for material used in this book, whether companies or individuals, have been obtained. Any omission is unintentional and we will be pleased to correct any errors in future editions of this book.

For More Information

Summit University Press books are available at fine bookstores worldwide and at your favorite on-line bookseller. For a free catalog of our books and products or to learn more about the spiritual techniques featured in this book, please contact:

Summit University Press
PO Box 5000, Corwin Springs, MT 59030-5000 USA
Tel: 1-800-245-5445 or 406-848-9500
Fax: 1-800-221-8307 or 406-848-9555
E-mail: info@summituniversitypress.com
www.summituniversitypress.com

Fallen Angels and the Origins of Evil

Why Church Fathers Suppressed
the Book of Enoch and
Its Startling Revelations

by Elizabeth Clare Prophet

**Did rebel angels take on
human bodies to fulfill
their lust for the "daughters
of men"?**

Did these fallen angels teach men
to build weapons of war? That is
the premise of the Book of Enoch,
a text cherished by the Essenes,

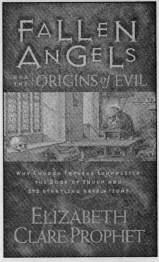

Pocketbook   524 pages $7.99
ISBN 0-922729-43-3

early Jews and Christians, but later condemned by both rabbis and
Church Fathers. The book was denounced, banned and "lost" for over
a thousand years—until in 1773 a Scottish explorer discovered three
copies in Ethiopia.

Elizabeth Clare Prophet examines the controversy surrounding
this book and sheds new light on Enoch's forbidden mysteries. She
demonstrates that Jesus and the apostles studied the book and tells why
Church Fathers suppressed its teaching that angels could incarnate in
human bodies.

Fallen Angels and the Origins of Evil takes you back to the primor-
dial drama of Good and Evil, when the first hint of corruption entered a
pristine world—earth.

Contains Richard Laurence's translation of the Book of Enoch,
all the other Enoch texts (including the Book of the Secrets of Enoch),
and biblical parallels. 12 illustrations.

SUMMIT UNIVERSITY 🕯 PRESS®
To order call 1-800-245-5445

Pocket Guides to Practical Spirituality

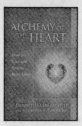

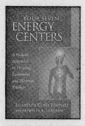

ELIZABETH CLARE PROPHET
is a world-renowned author and has
pioneered techniques in practical
spirituality, including the creative
power of sound for personal growth
and world transformation. Among
her bestsellers are *Fallen Angels and
the Origins of Evil, Karma and
Reincarnation* and *The Lost Years of
Jesus*. Since the 1960s, she has conducted seminars and
workshops worldwide on karma and reincarnation,
prophecy, soul mates, mysticism and angels.

PATRICIA R. SPADARO is coauthor
of *Karma and Reincarnation, Alchemy
of the Heart, Your Seven Energy Centers, The Art of Practical Spirituality*
and *Kabbalah: Key to Your Inner
Power*. Patricia specializes in practical
spirituality and mysticism, drawing on
all the world's great spiritual traditions.

MURRAY L. STEINMAN is a writer,
public speaker and specialist in strate-
gic communication. He is coauthor of
Kabbalah: Key to Your Inner Power
and has appeared on numerous radio
and TV shows, including *Oprah* and
Donahue.